CADES COVE:
A PERSONAL HISTORY

This is the place. Stand still, my steed,

Let me review the scene,

And summon from the shadowy Past

The forms that once have been.

—Longfellow

"Memory is the treasury and guardian of all things."

—Cicero

CADES COVE:

A PERSONAL HISTORY

BY

JUDGE WILLIAM WAYNE OLIVER

Published in the United States by Great Smoky Mountains Association.
Great Smoky Mountains Association is a private, nonprofit organization which supports the educational, scientific, and historical programs of Great Smoky Mountains National Park. Our publications are an educational service intended to enhance the public's understanding and enjoyment of the national park. If you would like to know more about our publications, memberships, guided hikes and other projects, please contact:

Great Smoky Mountains Association
P.O. Box 130
Gatlinburg, TN 37738
(865) 436-7318
www.SmokiesInformation.org

ISBN: 978-0-937207-79-6
Editors: Steve Kemp and Kent Cave
Illustration and book design: Joey Heath
Editorial assistance: Julie Brown and Cyn Slaughter
Photographs courtesy Julia Jane Oliver Webb, the Randolph Shields collection, and GSMNP archives
Printed in Hong Kong.

01 02 03 04 05 06 07 08 09

Contents

There is a Land in Tennessee

I know of a land in
Tennessee

Where the streams and the
mountains meet

And the moonbeams play
all night they say

In the brooks at the
mountains' feet,

Where tall peaks stand
sublime and grand

To guard the serenity of the
valleys below,

And wildcats prowl and the
lonesome owls

Chant their ceaseless
"Who-Who-ho, Who-Who-ho."

My Birthplace
—Origin of the Name

That land is Cades Cove, in Blount County, Tennessee, the land of my birth.

The origin of the name of this extraordinarily beautiful valley in the mountains of East Tennessee, subject of much speculation and myth, has been established definitively by the research of a nephew, Dr. Durwood Clay Dunn, head of the History Department of Tennessee Wesleyan College. In his UT doctoral dissertation entitled *Cades Cove in the Nineteenth Century*, he refers to the Tuckaleechee mercantile store records of his great-great-grandfather Peter Snyder's transactions with Cherokee Chief Kade, who was living in the Cove at the time of the initial white settlement there and was well known to the early settlers. Dr. Dunn also cites Robert Lindsay Mason's *The Lure of the Great Smokies* for the earliest correct published account of Chief Kade.

Unquestionably, by the passage of time and long usage, Kade's came to be spelled Cades. By reference to James Mooney's *Myths of the Great Smokies*, Dr. Dunn documents that the Cherokee name for Cades Cove was Tsiyahi, meaning otter place.

Some Family History and Reflections

*M*y great-great grandparents were John Oliver (1793-1864) and Lucretia (Lureny) Frazier Oliver (1795-1888). During the War of 1812, John enlisted in Captain Adam Winsell's Company of the Tennessee Militia on January 5, 1814, Colonel Ewen Allison's Regiment, under General Andrew Jackson. He fought under General Jackson in the battle of Horseshoe Bend on March 27, 1814. He was mustered out of service at Knoxville on May 26, 1814 and returned to his home in Carter County, Tennessee. He and Lucretia Frazier were married April 28, 1815, their first child was born in July, 1817. In 1818 they moved from Carter County to Cades Cove, to become the first permanent white settlers in the Cove. There had been a few white people coming and going prior to that time, but John and Lucretia Oliver were the first to come and stay and rear a family and make it their permanent home. By occupation, he was a farmer and collier [coal miner], and burned charcoal for early iron forges in the Cove. Forge Creek is so named because an iron forge was located on that stream. He helped organize and was a charter member of the first organized church in Cades Cove in 1827, which became the Primitive Baptist Church of Cades Cove. He and his wife and all their children are buried in the cemetery at that church, as are all my other ancestors and deceased members of my family, with the exception of one brother, Henry Clay Oliver, buried in the National Cemetery at Knoxville.

The first land owned by John Oliver in the Cove was 50 acres he bought September 22, 1826 from Issac Hart. (Deed Book 2, page 480, Register's Office of Blount County). On September 2, 1832 he bought 36 acres from Isaac Hart (Deed Book 5 page 101, Register's Office of Blount County). He next acquired 40 acres by Grant No. 3397 from the State of Tennessee,

This is the grave marker of John Oliver and Lucretia (Lureny) Frazier Oliver, my great-great grandparents. They were married April 28, 1815. In 1818 they moved from Carter County to Cades Cove to become the first permanent white settlers in the Cove.

dated July 6, 1839 which was never recorded. The original of that grant was given to my father, John W. Oliver by James R. (Jim) Oliver, 1879-1956, who was a son of William M. (Bill) Oliver, (see page 9).

It would seem reasonable to surmise that John Oliver built his first home in about 1826 or 1827, on his first tract of land in the Cove soon after its acquisition. That house was erected just above the present structure; a pile of rocks above the existing house marks the chimney location of the original one.

As descendants of Frederick Shields and Mary (Polly) Oliver, both Dr. A. Randolph Shields, retired Chairman of Maryville College Biology Department, and Maryville Mayor Stanley B. (Skeeter) Shields are great-great-grandsons of John and Lucretia Oliver.

Rutha Oliver, daughter of John and Lucretia Oliver, and Walter Gregory. Sometime after Walter passed away from measles during the Civil War, she married Nathan Burchfield.

My great-grandparents were Elijah Oliver and Mary (Polly) Lawson Oliver, sister of Squire Daniel B. Lawson, a large landowner and prominent citizen of the Cove. In an autobiographical account covering portions of his life, my grandfather William H. Oliver, son of Elijah, relates that he was "born in a little log house in the upper end of Cades Cove, Blount County, Tennessee on what was afterwards called the Harverson Branch about 1/4 mile above where Elder W. A. (Andy) Gregory last lived. Soon after I was born my parents moved to Tuckaleechee Cove near the foot of the Good Ridge. We lived there seven years, and moved back to the lower end of Cades Cove the day peace was made at the end of the Civil War in 1865. I was about eight years old at this time. Here I grew to manhood..." My father states in some of his historical writings that "During the Civil War his (Elijah's) sympathies were with the Union side. He, with a number of others in Cades Cove, never enlisted in the War but acted as a Home Guard. He was taken prisoner by the Rebels and put in a prison camp at Dandridge, Tennessee. But he escaped after several weeks and returned home, by night;" and that he spent all of his life in Cades Cove except for the period he lived in Tuckaleechee Cove.

The first land owned by Elijah Oliver in Cades Cove was 93.5 acres bought October 27, 1865 from John Anthony (Deed Book BB, page 289, Register's Office of Blount County). He next bought 40 acres on January 24, 1870 from Alfred McConnell, which joined his 93.5 acre tract, and was described as part of what was known as the William Davis tract. (Deed Book CC, page 331, Register's Office of Blount County). In January 1871 he acquired 120 acres from "John White, W. D. McGinley, John D. Alexander, Alfred McConnell, Moses McConnell, J. G. Bogel, James Matthews, J. G. Wells, Samuel D. Gaughron, G. T. Gates, and John W. Gates." This land is described as being in the lower end of Cades Cove "which when taken in connection with the 40 acre tract which the said Oliver now owns, forms a square which is one-half mile each way," and as bounded by William Davis and William Tipton (Deed Book EE, page 460, Register's Office of Blount County).

From the foregoing record of his land acquisitions, it appears fairly certain that Elijah Oliver built his first home in Cades Cove in 1865 and 1866 on his first tract of land bought from John Anthony, and moved into that home from Tuckaleechee Cove. Later he sold his property in Tuckaleechee (85 acres bought from G. W. Snyder in 1858, Deed Book BB, page 350) to George W. King on May 7, 1867 (Deed Book BB, page 358, Register's Office of Blount County). At the Elijah Oliver home place in Cades Cove is the only complete set of historic farm buildings still standing on the original site in Great Smoky Mountains National Park; they consist of the two-story dwelling house with a breezeway porch separating the kitchen from the remainder; the barn, the corn crib, the smoke house, and the spring-house. A blacksmith shop, which I remember very well, was removed many years ago when by deterioration it became unusable.

On December 2, 1904 Elijah Oliver conveyed 225 acres to his daughter

Elijah and Mary (Polly) Lawson Oliver were my paternal great-grandparents. She was the sister of Squire Daniel B. Lawson, a prominent citizen of the Cove.

Elizabeth Abbott, the deed description reciting "known as the Elijah Oliver place, which he bought from John Anthony, and part from a company of land holders" (Deed Book 59 page 201, Register's Office of Blount County). On January 21, 1907 Elizabeth Abbott and her daughter Mary J. Abbott sold to my father John W. Oliver the same 225 acres. (Deed Book 65 page 546, Register's Office of Blount County).

In his historical writings my father relates that although Elijah Oliver had only a few weeks of rudimentary education in what was called an Article of Subscription School (in which parents signed an agreement to help underwrite the contract-teacher's compensation by subscribing thereto on a pro-rata basis determined by the number of the subscriber's children attending), he learned to write "a very smooth hand" and served as church clerk and deacon of the original church of Cades Cove for thirty-seven years; and was a school director in the Sixteenth Civil District of Blount County (Cades Cove) for many years.

As a boy, I spent many nights in the Elijah home during the tenure of some of our tenants who lived there. At one time Mrs. Phoeba Wilson Snodgrass (who later married Uncle Jim Cable—the miller) and her daughters, Elsie and Ella Josephine lived there for a few years. Ella Josephine was the mother of Dr. A. Randolph Shields. Elsie married Paul Wilcox. During the early years of our marriage, my wife and I spent many weekends in that house while my parents still lived in the Cove. They had the house partially furnished suitable for tourist occupancy during the last several years they lived in the Cove. Mart (Martin) Tipton and his wife Elsie Shields Tipton and family lived in the Elijah house as tenants for a few years. Also, John A. Myers and Ella Rebecca Oliver Myers and family lived there for some time. And Jim Hatcher and wife Lydia Lawson Hatcher and family lived there several years, helping in the farming operations.

I have Elijah's billfold. In it are various papers, some pertaining to his duties as a school director. Also included is a pass issued by the Provost Marshall's Office at Knoxville on October 3, 1863, directing the guards to allow Elijah Oliver to pass through the lines on the Maryville road. On the reverse side appears the following, signed by him:

"Oath of Allegiance"

This is the Henry Whitehead home place.

"This Pass is given and taken with the condition that the bearer hereof solemnly swears to bear true faith and allegiance to the United States Government, and that he will conduct himself in all respects as a loyal citizen of said Government. For the faithful observance of this obligation he pledges his property and life."

My paternal grandparents were William Howell Oliver and Elizabeth Jane Gregory. As above indicated, grandfather Oliver was a son of Elijah and Mary (Polly) Lawson Oliver. Grandmother Oliver was born in Graham County, North Carolina, December 18, 1886, a daughter of Charles Garrison Gregory (1823-1900) and Celia Carver (1830-1906). Her grandparents were Russell Gregory (1795-1864) and Susan Hill (1796-1880).

Russell Gregory spent much time in the area of Gregory Bald, named after him. He and his wife Susan Hill, and Robert Burchfield and his wife Elizabeth Hill, were from Yancey County, North Carolina. Russell and his family first settled in Monroe County, Tennessee, but soon moved across the Little Tennessee River to Chilhowee near the Milligan Springs area. He and his oldest son, John, took a trip to Ringgold, Georgia to work in the mines, where the son became ill and died as they were en route home, and his father buried him at Chilhowee. In about 1835 Russell Gregory and his family moved to Cades Cove. In my father's historical writings he fixes that date from the old church records showing that some of Russell Gregory's children appeared on the membership roll in 1837. In his book, *The Families of Cades Cove*, Dr. Randolph Shields says

Jim Hatcher and wife Lydia Lawson Hatcher and family lived at the Elijah Oliver home place for several years, helping in the farming operations.

that Russell Gregory first appeared on the Census record of 1850. After settling his family on land he acquired in Cades Cove, he obtained an entry to several thousand acres of mountain land in both Tennessee and north North Carolina, including what became known as Gregory Bald; built a cabin and developed this land into a stock ranch for grazing livestock, and spent the summer months there many years as a rancher and herdsman. It is said he would blow a large horn (made from a cow horn) which cattle recognized, to call them from the coves and hollows to the mountain top to give them salt. On the bald he constructed a round stone enclosure in which he would conceal himself on moonlit nights and kill deer for meat when they were attracted to salt placed nearby for cattle.

Father also relates that Russell Gregory's right hand was amputated because of a serious infection to his right thumb by a man who challenged

Home.

Small barn.

him to fight, during which Russell chewed the man's ear off and broke his challenger's hold on his thumb; and that thereafter Russell wore a metal hook attached to his right wrist. When the Civil War erupted his sympathies were with the Union, but being too old for military service he organized a Home Guard of elderly men of like sentiments to protect the women and children in the community. One of his sons joined the Union forces and another went into the Confederate army, an example of the historical division of families resulting from that conflict. On one occasion

Barn.

This set of buildings was the home of my great-grandparents Elijah and Mary (Polly) Oliver.

Corn crib.

he and other members of the Home Guard waited in the lower end of the cove on the Happy Valley Road to intercept a North Carolina raiding party, who made several plundering forays in Cades Cove confiscating whatever they wanted. When the Home Guard fired on them, rebel raiders retreated, abandoning the livestock they had taken, and left the cove by a different route. One member of that raiding party was one of Russell Gregory's sons who recognized his father's rifle–"Old Long Tom." A few weeks later, some members of the same raiding party returned to the cove, and under cover

*My grandfather William Howell Oliver with his second wife Elizabeth Jane Gregory
Oliver. She was the granddaughter of Russell Gregory,
for whom Gregory Bald is named.*

of darkness forced their way into Russell Gregory's home and murdered
him as he arose from his bed. On his grave marker in the Primitive Baptist
Cemetery is the statement, "Murdered by North Carolina Rebels." He and

his wife were my great-great-grandparents.

The home of grandfather and grandmother Oliver is located on the south side of Cades Cove, now the next homestead on the loop road beyond the Dan Lawson place. In the current guide, this home of my grandparents is called the Tipton Place, with no mention of the fact this was the William H. Oliver home. In 1875 a carpenter named Jackie Stephenson built the original house for Colonel J. W. Hamp Tipton, who had it built for his daughter, Louisa Katherine and son-in-law Patterson (Pat) Dunn. To this couple a son, Claude Dunn—whom I remember well—was born. Pat Dunn died there, and his widow and son left Cades Cove when Claude was three years old. My father, John W. Oliver, son of William H. Oliver, has told me many times that they moved to this home from the Carter Shields place when he was nine years old. My father was born October 14, 1878, so this means that his parents moved to this home in 1887. There they raised their family, and grandfather Oliver continued to live there until after his property was acquired for Great Smoky Mountains National Park. He expanded the house to meet the needs of a growing family, adding about a fifteen-foot extension on the end next to the road, and a room onto the end of the kitchen, and constructed grain bins upstairs for storage. He also built a bee shed directly above the house, a springhouse (now gone), a smoke house, shop and barn. For a number of years he operated a mercantile store. I recall the store building, with its wide white pine paneling and shelves. That building was located about fifty yards directly south of the shop. In the right wall of the kitchen will be seen two small wooden boxes, each with a small hole in the bottom or outside surface. Two like boxes were located in the store. A piece of rawhide was attached by wood pegs to cover the holes on the inside of the boxes. By stretching small wire from the boxes in the kitchen to those in the store, constant communication was possible. It is amazing how well this telephone system worked for the distance of about two hundred yards.

Some of my fondest memories are of times at grandfather Oliver's house.

Quite often, especially when apples
and grapes were ripe, a host of
grandchildren and parents would
gather there, usually on Sunday,
to visit with our grandparents and
with each other. These were joyous
occasions. In my youth I frequently
spent a night with grandfather and
grandmother Oliver. They were very
devout Christians. They took turns
conducting the family devotions,
reading a selection from the Bible
and praying. How well I remember
those occasions, all kneeling in
front of the hearth.

*The gravestone of Russell Gregory,
my great-great-grandfather.*

Grandfather Oliver was ordained as a Primitive Baptist Minister on
August 27, 1882 and served actively for over fifty years in the Cades Cove
church, and also in other communities—to which he rode horseback or
walked. He was a gifted singer and could sing many of the old hymns from
memory, and could quote whole chapters in the Bible. By occupation he
was a farmer, blacksmith, furniture maker, merchant for a number of years,
and was also a shoemaker. He made some of the shoes for his family, and I
can recall seeing him with a pair he built for himself. Although his formal
schooling totaled about twelve months, according to my father, he wrote a
very legible hand and was considerably well-read and abreast of the times.

Grandfather and grandmother Oliver came to our house on December 24,
1924 to spend Christmas. Early Christmas morning, grandmother suffered a
severe stroke while walking in the yard. She died on January 5, 1925.

After the death of his wife, grandfather Whitehead's family Bible records
that he married Matilda Shields Gregory, 1843–1924, on August 12, 1887,

Andy Gregory and sons with Russell Gregory's rifle. The rifle is said to be the first gun fired in the Civil War in Cades Cove.

and moved with his three small daughters to Cades Cove from the Crooked Creek community near Maryville in the fall of 1887. Matilda was a daughter of Frederick and Mary (Polly) Oliver Shields. Her first husband, Ebenezer Gregory, had deserted her and their small son Josiah Jonathan Gregory, known in the cove as "Joe Banty" Gregory because of his short stature. In 1870–1933 Dr. A. Randolph Shields has recorded that Ebenezer was also called (Azer) and remarried in Texas after leaving Matilda who then divorced him (*The Families of Cades Cove*, 1921–1936, pages 201, 423).

In 1893 grandfather Whitehead built a log house connected by a breezeway porch to Matilda's one-room log house, which then became the kitchen. The three girls were now teenagers. Aunt Jane, born September 9, 1876, was then 17; Nancy Ann, born September 15, 1878, was then 15; and Aunt Susan, born July 2, 1880, was then 13. Those girls made the bricks for the chimney of their new home. This chimney was refaced with new bricks by the National Park Service only a few years ago to

This is the John Oliver cabin.

shield the original bricks which had begun to show deterioration. With that modification, that house and Matilda's are still preserved as the Henry Whitehead place, which is located about a mile straight ahead from the Cable Mill intersection, and is visited by countless people.

The family was living in that house at the time my father and mother were married on September 4, 1901, when they were almost 23 years old. Grandfather Whitehead lived there the remainder of his life. In his active years he was a farmer, beekeeper, and avid hunter. I have seen the remains of his wild turkey pen in the Lick Log Branch area of the Smoky Mountains, some five or six miles from his home. This pen, eight or nine feet square, was constructed of small logs and was about five feet high and covered with logs. On one side a trench was dug—large enough and sufficiently deep for a turkey to walk in—extending from a few feet outside to a short distance inside the pen. About two feet of the trench just inside were covered. Shelled corn was scattered in the trench from end to end. Turkeys eating the corn found themselves inside the pen; then trying to

Two small wooden boxes, each with a small hole in the bottom or outside surface were attached inside the house in the kitchen. Two like boxes were located in the store. By stretching a small wire from the boxes in the kitchen to those in the store, constant communication was possible.

escape, they ran around the inside walls of the pen without stepping in the trench or looking down to find the way out. Mother has told me about going to check the turkey pen. She became a very accomplished cook of all kinds of wild game.

Grandfather Whitehead gave me his box-type turkey caller and his double-spring steel trap and broad axe, and his trundle bed. From my earliest recollection of him he was incapacitated and bedridden with rheumatism and was unable to care for his bees or do any other work. As a child I often visited him and slept in a trundle bed which, when not in use, was kept under his high-posted bed. That bed is a prized possession. He had many colonies of bees, housed in a bee shed on the hill facing the house. A chore delegated to me was to sit on the breezeway porch and keep watch on the bees during swarming time and see where the young swarms settled, on an apple tree limb or elsewhere nearby. My father was the rural mail carrier in the Cove, and at that time his route schedule was such that he got to grandfather Whitehead's about noon each day, where he stopped to have lunch and feed his horse. He would hive the swarm of bees.

Of course, except for the small area in the immediate vicinity of the house, all of the Henry Whitehead farm has long since completely reverted

19

*My maternal grandfather, Henry Whitehead, married Sarah Margaret Boring. After
her death he married Matilda Shields Gregory, shown above with daughter Jane.
Matilda was the daughter of Frederick Shields and Mary Oliver Shields.*

to forest. After grandfather Whitehead died, Matilda lived the rest of her
life with Aunt Jane and Uncle Russell D. Burchfield.

My parents were John Walter Oliver and Nancy Ann Whitehead Oliver.
He grew up in Cades Cove and attended the public schools a few weeks

each year, and at the age of 21 completed the fifth grade. He stayed at home with his parents, working on the farm to help with the rearing of his younger brothers and sisters, until he reached the age of 21. In September 1899 he entered the preparatory department of Maryville College. He and three other young men, including Granville Dexter LeQuire, 1879–1960, also born in Cades Cove, rented and occupied a small two-room cottage located about where the Caldwell Fence Company's fenced storage lot is now situated on the Sevierville Road (U.S. 411). Much of their food was furnished by their families, and they "batched" there, doing their own cooking and housekeeping while attending Maryville College. Granville Dexter LeQuire later became a medical doctor. I was the first child he delivered after completion of his medical education and was licensed to practice medicine.

At the end of his first term at Maryville College, my father secured a county certificate to teach school. Beginning in the fall of 1900 he taught school in a one-room school house in the upper or east end of Cades Cove, which was located about fifty yards east of where Sparks Lane crosses the creek. His teaching salary was $23.00 per month. At the end of that term, he returned to Maryville College in the spring of 1901. In the fall of the same year he again began teaching school in the Cove. In September 1902, after he and mother were married, he entered Maryville College again for further study. After teaching in the Cove school another term in the fall and early winter of 1903–1904, he and mother went to Louisville, Kentucky in January 1904 where he entered Massey Business College. Graduating there in August, 1901, they returned to Cades Cove.

My father's second marriage was to Florence Whitehead Tucker (1880 –1967), widow of the late John Tucker of Maryville.

A note in my father's own hand, attached to an early photograph of him and my mother, reads as follows;

This photograph was taken at Maryville, Tennessee, on

My mother and father were married on September 4, 1901, when they were almost 23 years old.

Saturday afternoon of January 26, 1901. Next day, Sunday, Nancy Ann and I rode horseback all the way from Maryville through the flats of the Chilhowee Mountains to Cades Cove, a distance of 20 miles, without ever dismounting from our horses. It was a cold blue day but our hearts were warm for each other. I had on the first whole suit of clothes I ever owned. I bought them on Saturday, January 26, 1901 with the first money I

Beginning in the fall of 1900 and for three years hence, my father taught school in a one-room school house in Cades Cove. His salary was $23.00 per month.

ever earned teaching school at $23.00 per month; they cost me $8.50. We were 22 years old and not married. We were married September 4, 1901. John W. Oliver.

After they returned from Louisville, Kentucky, my parents lived for a few years on a small mountain farm owned by grandfather Oliver and known as "Brown's Hollow," because this tract had been owned previously by Levi Bennett Brown, son-in-law of Elijah and Mary (Polly) Lawson Oliver. This farm was located about 1.5 miles south of grandfather Oliver's home, well up against the side of the mountain. The house was a two-room log structure with a lean-to kitchen. That is where Irene and I were born. Much later it was also the home of Aunt Ruth Hassell Oliver Taylor and her husband George Taylor for a few of the early years of their marriage.

My sister, Irene Ryan was born February 7, 1905 and died of diphtheria on September 22, 1907. I was born August 11, 1907 and also contracted the disease. My father sent for a Dr. Jenkins, who lived at Townsend, Tennessee. He came with the then new wonder medicine called diphtheria antitoxin; it was too late to save little Irene, but it saved my life. I still bear the scar on the left side of my neck where the doctor lanced my swollen throat.

The Fisher Place

This is my aunt, Frances Oliver Shields, and her children Herman, in back, and from the right, Nola, Sue, Norma, and Flaura. Herman was witness to my fascination with hornets' nests.

Leaving "Brown's Hollow" in August or September of 1908, my parents moved to a twenty-five acre farm located east of and adjoining grandfather Oliver's property, from whom they bought it on August 21, 1908. (Deed Book 73 page 367 Register's Office of Blount County). It lays on both sides of the loop road, beginning at the first hilltop going east from grandfather's home. My very first recollections center on this place, known as the Fisher Place, because one Frank Fisher had lived there. The two-room log house was on the right side of the road at the eastern edge of this property. I can remember when Preacher W. A. (Andy) Gregory built us a barn on the other side of the road and about fifty yards west of the house. I can also remember well the time when my cousin Herman Shields and I found a large hornet's nest on the bank of the road near our house. I hit upon the imprudent idea of closing the nest by inserting a corn cob into the plainly visible access hole. After getting Herman well back from the danger zone, I inserted the cob. Little did I know that the hornets also had a back door, but that became apparent at once when they swarmed out of that entrance and attacked me. I at once made a strategic withdrawal as fast as I could run, but several of the enraged hornets gave me their best shots.

In the 1920s father had a silo built onto the rear of the barn at the Fisher Place, which was filled with corn grown in those fields, and we wintered several cattle there on the silage. Herman and Uncle Andrew Shields, who lived on the adjoining farm, did the feeding. But since we then lived in the lower end of the Cove, continuation of that program proved to be impractical and it was abandoned after a few years. On the left of the road and just beyond the first branch east of grandfather Oliver's house, and about fifty yards beyond our Fisher Place home, stands a magnificent white oak tree. The home of Aunt Frances and Uncle Andrew Shields was located on the slope of the hill opposite that tree. Their large farm extended into the hills on the south side of the road and all the way to Abrams Creek on the north side. Well do I remember the very productive grove of chestnut trees they had. When we lived at the Fisher Place, my mother carried water from their spring, and used their wash-place to do her laundering.

Establishment of Daily Mail Delivery

My father on his daily mail route.

n September of 1904, my father took and passed the U. S. Civil Service postal examination, establishment of mail service in Cades Cove having been approved. He received appointment as the first rural mail carrier in Cades Cove, in which capacity he served continuously for thirty-five years. This was the beginning of rural free mail delivery (RDF) in the Cove.

The first postmaster after rural free mail delivery was established was Andrew Witt Shields, Sr., 1860–1919, a son of William Henry H. Shields and Martha Oliver Shields. Uncle Witt Shields owned and operated a large successful farm and was a leader in the community. His wife, Aunt Mary, actually conducted the day to day business of the post office. I can remember both of them very well. Uncle Witt had an inventive mind. He built a washing machine, operated from a power take-off from his water-powered grist mill. It was reported that Aunt Mary got her hand caught in the washing machine and narrowly escaped injury. They owned the finest home in

At one time the Cades Cove Post Office was at the home of Murray T. Boring (above left), which was located on the NW side of the Cove, past the Missionary Baptist Church.

Murray Boring (back row, far left) with his wife and children.

the cove. After about ten years, the post office was moved to the lower end of the cove, and Jonathan Wade Hampton Myers became the postmaster. He set up the post office in a partitioned section in the rear of his store. After the death of Jonathan Myers in 1924, his brother-in-law, Murray T. Boring, 1896-1974, a World War I veteran who married Cordia Myers, 1899-1980, became Cades Cove's last Postmaster.

Andrew Witt Shields was my dad's uncle by marriage, and postmaster.

28

Move to Lower End of Cove

(Property Improvements)

My mother, Nancy Ann, holding Winston, with me and Lucille in the back row and Geneva and Clay in the front row. This photo was taken at Webb Studios in Maryville in May 1920.

On December 18, 1911, my parents bought a tract of land from John Sparks and wife in the lower end of Cades Cove. (Deed Book 73, page 369, Register's Office of Blount County). This land joined the Elijah Oliver tract father bought from Elizabeth and Mary J. Abbott in January, 1907, as already noted. We moved to this Sparks property in December, 1911.

This is the concrete box my father built for keeping milk and butter cool.

During the next several years this house was greatly improved and remodeled. A combination corn crib and tool house, and a granary (with a large cellar underneath) were built, as well as a blacksmith shop, and a 100-foot-long bee shed to house the bees acquired from grandfather Whitehead. We dug a well near the kitchen, eliminating the considerable inconvenience of carrying water from the nearest spring, which was at the foot of the hill about 100 yards from the house. Father had earlier improved the spring with a two-section concrete box (one for water and the other for keeping milk and butter, etc.) and a spring house. The kitchen was added during the remodeling.

In 1919 my father hired two Cove men, Lazarus Anthony and J. Witt Roberts, who owned a sawmill outfit and were partners in the lumbering and building business, and who had done the remodeling of our house, to saw lumber cut from our land and build a new barn and silo. Manuel Ledbetter brought his small portable steam engine and planing machine to dress the lumber for the barn. My father and I hauled 30-foot two–by-fours to the Little River Lumber Company plant at Townsend to have them tongued and grooved for the silo. This required extending the wagon to the

This is our final home in Cades Cove. We cut timber from our land and had Lazarus Anthony and J. Witt Roberts dress the wood.

maximum length of twenty feet and using two teams of horses.

It was dark long before we got home, and I remember how I marveled at father's skill in handling that long wagon and the two teams around all the sharp turns in the mountain road in the dark, although surely his and the horses' eyes became somewhat adjusted to the darkness. The new red barn and silo were completed in 1920. The barn, still standing (1984) on its concrete foundation, is 40 feet x 72 feet. The silo was 12 feet in diameter, thirty feet high above ground and 10 feet deep below ground level. We were all so proud of our new barn and silo, great assets in the care and feeding of our cattle in winter. We grew a combination of corn and sorghum cane for silage, and filling the silo and putting up hay were annual operations.

Ranging Livestock
and the End of the World

n early May of each year, we took most of our cattle to the mountain range for the summer. We sent along a few older dry (non-lactating) cows every year as leaders, those that had been to the mountain before. They knew well where they were going when bells were put on them and the others that were going to the mountain. When the drive started those old cows got in front, eager to go. We always took our cattle above the "Marion Field," so named because Marion Burchfield cleared some thirty or forty acres and lived there a number of years long before my time. This area was in a valley just east of the Fork Ridge and below the Gant Lot. To reach the place we drove up the Ekaneetlee Creek trail to the famous Big Poplar. There we turned right on a trail leading to the Marion Field. Of course, the cattle gradually worked their way out to the top of the mountain, and to other parts of the range. No trace of the Marion Field remains.

The range extended several miles on both sides of the top of Smoky Mountain (the Tennessee-North Carolina state line) from Parson Bald to the Lawson Gant Lot, which is about four or five miles east of Ekaneetlee Gap. The Lawson Gant Lot was a large level grassland of about a hundred acres where Squire Daniel B. Lawson corralled his cattle at the end of the range season. It is said his land once extended across Cades Cove from the state line on the south to the top of Cades Cove Mountain on the north. We used to take our sheep to the Lawson Gant Lot.

Many other people in the Cove, and several farmers from other areas of Blount County, sent cattle and sheep to the mountain. Mr. Charlie Proffitt, who owned a farm near Maryville, once stopped at our house en route to the mountain with his sheep which he had driven in on the Cooper Road. One ewe had twin lambs, one of which she rejected. Knowing it would not survive on the mountain, Mr. Proffitt gave that lamb to me. It was no trick to teach it to suck a young black cow we had whose teats were so small it was difficult to milk her. With that nourishment he grew rapidly. It didn't take much teasing to teach him to butt. Uncle Hamp Myers bought him for a herd sire, by then a full grown buck. One day, finding Uncle Hamp in a stooped position scattering salt for the sheep, this buck was unable to resist the opportunity; he charged from the rear and turned him head over heels down the hillside.

Two men, not always the same individuals, would lease a large area on the Tennessee side from Morton Butler Lumber Company (a Chicago based firm which owned some 29,000 acres of mountain land), and also an extensive area on the North Carolina side from Kitchen Lumber Company, for livestock grazing. These men, called herders, would look after the cattle and sheep placed in their charge by the owners. Their fee was $1.00 per head for cattle if the owner furnished salt, and $1.50 if the herders provided the salt. For sheep the fee was either twenty-five or fifty cents per head, determined on the same basis. Sheep ranged along the top of the mountain for the most part, where there was an abundance of grass and very little underbrush; consequently, sheep gave the herders very little trouble. Cattle, on the other hand, ranged widely and required more work by the herders to keep track of them. The owners placed bells on many of their cattle, which enabled the herders to become familiar with each owner's bells and to be able to locate the general area where they were at a given time. The herders always had a cabin where they lived while on the mountain. Made of logs, with two bunks in the rear, a chimney and fireplace, one door, the roof (gable or shed type) covered with handmade shingles, the cabin was a rough but adequately comfortable structure. It was always located as near as possible to a good spring. Cooking was done on the fireplace, using a Dutch oven, kettles and frying pans and sauce pans. Provisions had to be kept in boxes or other containers to guard against the ravages of mice and

My brothers Hugh and Winston along with Otis Tipton helping out around the farm.

squirrels and chipmunks, since the cabin was by no means rodent proof. All food items were brought from home by the herders. I recall three different cabins. One was on the Tennessee side, at a spring on the west side of the Fork Ridge, about half a mile below the top of the mountain. Both the others were on the North Carolina side. One was located in a small cleared area about a mile from the Gant Lot; the other was at Rye Patch, then an open area of several acres.

The herding season ended on Labor Day. During the preceding week the herders rounded up all the cattle and placed them in a corral of approximately 100 acres, fenced with chestnut logs. There was one spring in this enclosure. By the time a few hundred head of cattle remained here several days and ate all the grass, they became somewhat gaunt, or "gant" as some pronounced the word. Hence, this field or corral came to be called the Gant Lot and is so known to this day.

It was located on the top of the mountain about two and a half miles east of Gregory Bald and slightly east of where Fork Ridge reaches the top of the mountain.

On Labor Day, cattle owners or their representatives went to the Gant Lot. The herders would sort out an owner's cattle and give him a head start of a few minutes down the Fork Ridge toward the cove. That process continued until all the cattle were thus delivered to their owners. By mid-afternoon the sound of the cattle bells could be heard for half a mile before they came into view. Owners who lived outside the cove stopped at Uncle Noah Burchfield's home for the night and

Dave Sparks, the brother of Tom Sparks, herded cattle in Spence Field and Russell Field.

put their cattle in his meadows, resuming their journey the next morning.

Occasionally, a few cattle on the range contracted a disease known as "milk sick," which usually showed up at the end of the first day's drive off of the mountain. It was not uncommon for one or two to die in Uncle Noah's meadows. His large farm was across the road from ours. It was thought that the cattle which came down with "milk sick" or "milk sickness" were among those that wandered into the lowland areas along creeks far down on the North Carolina side. One such suspect area was a place called Tommys Cove. One summer my father sent me to spend a few days with herder Sam Sparks at the Rye Patch, and help drive some cattle, including some of ours, out of the Tommys Cove area. I remember that experience as a difficult and toilsome operation, which involved locating and collecting all the cattle in that area and driving them up Twenty Mile Ridge to the top of the mountain. Tommys Cove is now covered by

Cattle with bells.

Hugh Oliver at a herders' cabin.

Fontana Lake. The American Heritage Dictionary of the English Language says this about milk sickness: "1. An acute disease characterized by trembling, vomiting, and severe intestinal pain. It is caused by eating the dairy products or flesh of cattle poisoned by eating white snakeroot. 2. A disease

Clay and Frank Oliver.

Barn with added silo.

of cattle, the trembles." The same dictionary says of trembles; "Poisoning of domestic animals, especially cattle and sheep, caused by eating white snakeroot. Also called "milk sickness." This all agrees generally with Great Smoky Mountains Park Naturalist R. Glenn Cardwell, who says that in his native Greenbrier Cove, the offending snakeroot was called staggerweed. In the dictionary it is referred to as "staggerbush," defined as "A shrub...of the eastern United States, having poisonous foliage."

On the eastern end of the range, Tom Sparks herded cattle in the area of Spence Place and Russell Field for many years. He and his brother Dave Sparks owned those two places, each encompassing extensive acreage, much of it cleared and in grass. They had a large barn at Russell Field which they filled with hay cut there each year, and wintered some of their cattle. People in the east end of the cove and from Tuckaleechee Cove and Sevier County took cattle and sheep to that part of the range. The Sparks cabin was at the Spence Place. Tom stayed there much of the time in winter caring for their cattle, as well as in the summer when their own cattle and livestock sent to the range had to be kept up with and cared for. In 1926 he was shot and killed at the cabin by a disgruntled young man by the name of Earl Cameron, whom he had befriended and employed as a helper.

In the late 1920s, there was a period of about three or four years in which there was no herder on the mountain. In that circumstance, my father and my younger brothers built a cabin on the Tennessee side of the mountain about a mile east of the Gant Lot, arrangements for ranging his cattle having been made. During the summer for a couple of years or more, my brothers Henry Clay, Hugh, Winston, and cousin Frank Oliver, stayed in that cabin and looked after the cattle. It was constructed with a gable roof. I visited the boys there a couple of times. They usually went home on weekends to replenish their food supplies.

One afternoon in early June after my father got home from his route, he and I took a few cows and calves to range in the Licklog Branch area, which is good grazing territory some two miles north of Ekaneetlee Gap. To reach that section we drove them up what was known as the Mollys Butt Trail. It was past sundown by the time we reached the place to release the cattle. After eating some sandwiches mother had prepared for us we started home. It was getting dark by then. Coming down the Mollys Butt Trail, we noticed a very large ray of light sweeping across the sky. When we reached Uncle Russ Burchfield's house, Aunt Jane and her neighbor Aunt Jane Moody Shields were out in the yard looking at the great light; having never seen anything like that, they were wrought-up and felt sure the end of time was imminent. Uncle Russ had gone to Maryville that day, and came walking up the road during the excitement. At Maryville he had learned that a carnival show was going to demonstrate their great new searchlight that night. The apprehensive women were greatly relieved.

"Work Alone is Noble"
—Carlyle

My father, John Oliver, delivering mail in his Model T on Parson Branch Road.

e all worked hard on the farm. My father's mail route of almost twenty-four miles, on horseback or in a buggy, took about all day, especially in winter. In the summer he got home in time to do some work in the fields or with the bees. In his last several years as mail carrier he used an A-Model Ford when weather and road conditions were favorable.

Our days began at 4:00 a.m., winter and summer. My first chore was to start a fire in the kitchen stove for mother to prepare breakfast; in winter I also built a fire in the living room heater. Then I went to the barn and fed the horses. After breakfast father left on his mail route; then came the milking, feeding the cows and beginning the work of the day. In winter all the cattle were fed hay and silage both morning and night. Mother and

John Oliver plowing his field.

Lucile always helped with the milking and feeding. During the school term, all these chores had to be finished before starting the two mile walk to school; and the same routine was repeated after getting home from school.

Also, in the winter, from about November until March, I would set a trap line for muskrats along the creek. After feeding the horses, I would carry a lantern to check my traps, remove any rats caught and reset the traps. All pelting was done before going to school. The first money I ever made was from sale of muskrat pelts. Fox, minks, and coons, now plentiful in the Cove, were scarce in those days and I was never lucky enough to catch any of those.

Mills and Millers

Front row: John Robert (Bob) Cable (1871-1956), holding Nora Ellen Cable (1899-), Mary C. Ledbetter Cable (1879-1930) holding Jesse H. Cable (1901-1968), James V. Cable (1849-1930), Susan E. Burchfield (d. 1911). Back row: Laura Alice Cable (1896-1931) and Susan Angeline Cable, daughters of Bob Cable. The other three are children of James V. Cable.

Uncle Jim (James V.) Cable was the miller from my earliest recollection. He lived about a quarter of a mile up the creek from the mill. A bell mounted on a high pole was provided to summon him if he was not at the mill when a customer arrived. He also had a small shack with a rough stone chimney and fireplace, located opposite from the mill, where customers could keep warm while waiting their turn in winter. At the end of the walk leading into the mill, there were three large blocks of wood of different heights, arranged to form three steps. When my grist was

This is the warming shed at Cable Mill. Customers could keep warm while they waited for their grinding to get done.

finished and he was tying the sack, Uncle Jim would say, "Boy, get your nag." When I led my horse alongside the highest block, he would bring the sack, with the meal properly divided for balance, and put it on the horse; and from the same block it was easy to mount. He had a half-peck measure which he filled as his "toll" or charge for grinding a bushel of corn. Aunt Jane Moody also operated a grist mill, which many people patronized; it was known that she was a very capable miller and produced excellent meal. When that mill practically ceased operation in the late 1920s, my father bought it and set it up at our home, where he operated it with a Fordson tractor and ground corn for the family and neighbors. He moved the mill to Townsend when they moved out of the cove, and operated it there for a few years. After my parents passed away, we loaned the mill to Herbert Myers, of Townsend. Since the building it was housed in was fast deteriorating, Herbert agreed to use and preserve it until such time as we may desire to take it back.

A Cades Cove boy taking grain to the mill in the 1920s.

Cable Mill. John V. Cable, who was the brother of Becky Cable, ran the Cable Mill.

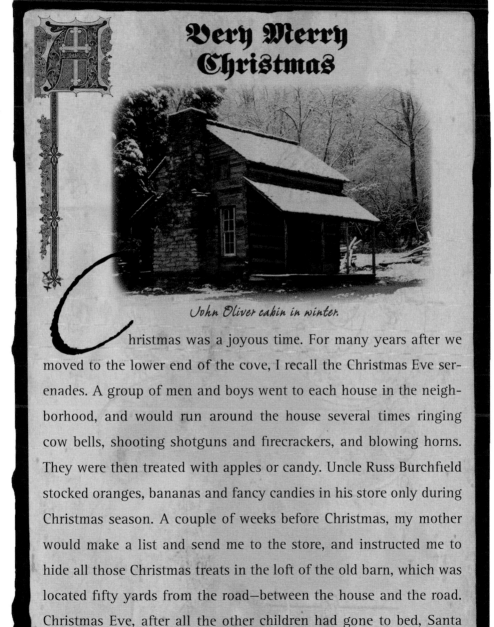

A Very Merry Christmas

John Oliver cabin in winter.

Christmas was a joyous time. For many years after we moved to the lower end of the cove, I recall the Christmas Eve serenades. A group of men and boys went to each house in the neighborhood, and would run around the house several times ringing cow bells, shooting shotguns and firecrackers, and blowing horns. They were then treated with apples or candy. Uncle Russ Burchfield stocked oranges, bananas and fancy candies in his store only during Christmas season. A couple of weeks before Christmas, my mother would make a list and send me to the store, and instructed me to hide all those Christmas treats in the loft of the old barn, which was located fifty yards from the road—between the house and the road. Christmas Eve, after all the other children had gone to bed, Santa Claus filled the stockings with the goodies from Uncle Russ's store. They were all up before daylight the next morning to see what Santa had brought.

A Leader in the Community

*M*y father was always a leader in the community. He introduced the first thoroughbred chickens (Rhode Island Reds), the first improved strain of bees (Three Banded Italians), the first thoroughbred hogs (Berkshire), the first thoroughbred sheep (Shropshire and Southdown), and the first thoroughbred cattle (Black Aberdeen Angus). The first Black Angus bull was purchased from the late Mr. John Hitch, who lived near Maryville and was one of the early pioneers in Tennessee with that breed. That first bull was named Ol' Black Joe. Cooperating with the county agent and the home demonstration agent, father helped organize boys' and girls' clubs in the Cove to assist them in learning improved farming and homemaking methods, on the order of present day Future Farmers of America.

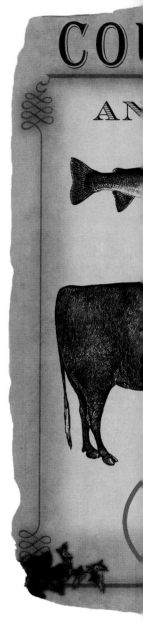

Father learned about caponizing (castrating) young roosters to improve their growth and also enhance their meat quality. He bought a set of caponizing tools and performed the operation on all excess young roosters when they reached about a pound and a half. They grew rapidly to very large size, never crowed and did not develop spurs. They brought premium prices when dressed in winter and shipped to Philadelphia or Washington, D.C. It is the same principle involved in castrating sheep, hogs, and cattle. Father also learned to vaccinate hogs to immunize against cholera, and cattle and sheep to prevent black-leg. He immunized our own animals, and those of neighbors who wanted the protection.

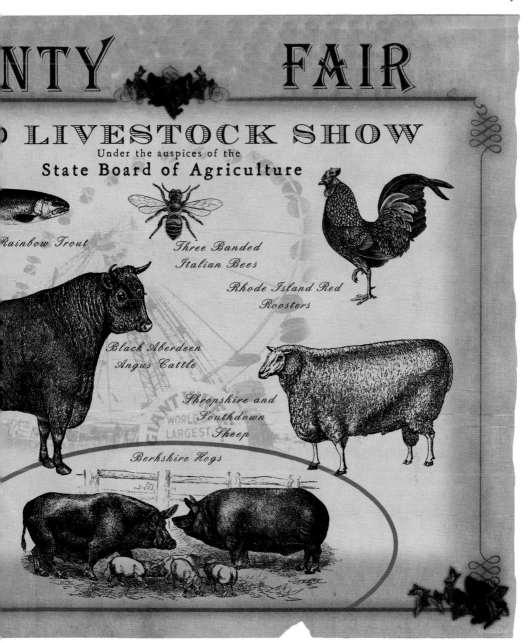

NTY   FAIR

LIVESTOCK SHOW
Under the auspices of the
State Board of Agriculture

Rainbow Trout

*Three Banded
Italian Bees*

*Rhode Island Red
Roosters*

*Black Aberdeen
Angus Cattle*

*Shropshire and
Southdown
Sheep*

Berkshire Hogs

My father bought the first grain binder in the cove, a far cry indeed from the old method of cutting grain with a scythe and cradle, the method employed to cut our first crop of wheat. Well do I remember watching that operation, four men going through the field in tandem formation—each cutting a swath about three feet wide and lifting the grain of each cut from

John Oliver with his bees.

Hugh Oliver with Otis Tipton.

the wooden fingers of the cradle and laying it in bunches on the ground. A man following behind tied the bunches into bundles—using a few pieces of grain twisted together—which were then formed into shocks by standing a number of bundles on end together. The shocks were sealed with a couple of bundles placed crosswise on top to protect the grain from rain. The new binder, in addition to vastly increasing the speed of cutting the grain, tied the bundles with twine and discharged them in groups of four or five in a place. This greatly facilitated shocking. After the grain was thoroughly

48

Nancy Oliver, in the background, with the cows.

Some of our chicken houses.

dry, the shocks were hauled to and stored in the barn loft. A threshing machine, powered by Manuel Ledbetter's portable steam engine, made the rounds through the cove in late summer threshing the grain. People who used straw in their bed ticks, as my family did, always took advantage of threshing time to wash and refill them with the clean yellow straw.

Father put the first rainbow trout in the streams of Cades Cove. Mr. Morton Butler, head of the Morton Butler Lumber Company mentioned earlier, had a summer cabin located on the hill just to the left of the en-

49

My mother, Nancy Ann Oliver, holding Lucille.

trance to Parson Branch Road, where he and friends spent a few summer weeks in the early years of the 20th century. He often rode with my father to the Chestnut Flats and back. Once in about 1905 he inquired about fish in the mountain streams. Father told him there were a few brook trout, the origin of which was unknown, and some horny-heads. Mr. Butler suggested enlisting the assistance of our congressman in getting rainbow trout fingerlings to stock the streams of the Cove. Judge Henry R. Gibson was in Congress at that time. He had written Gibson's Suits in Chancery, which is still the bible of equity practice in Tennessee. Father wrote to Judge Gibson, with the result that a few thousand rainbow trout fingerlings were shipped to Townsend from the fish hatchery at Erwin, Tennessee. When the fish arrived at the Townsend depot, the station agent, Uncle Enos Coulter, dispatched a post card to my father announcing their arrival. That required one day for father to get the card. By the time wagons could be sent to Townsend the following day, the release time stamped on the barrels had expired. So Uncle Enos had the fish dumped into Little River, across the road from the depot, as he was required to do under the circumstances. Those were the first rainbow trout in Little River. That was in 1907, the year I was born.

The next year, 1908, Judge Gibson arranged for another shipment of fingerling rainbows to be sent to Townsend, which was better coordinated. The wagons got there in time, and these fish were placed in Abrams Creek, across the road from our meadows, and in Post Creek.

The people of the Cove looked askance at this experiment, regarding it as another of John Oliver's newfangled ideas, like his thoroughbred chickens. Speculating that when the spring rains came all those fish would be washed over Abrams Falls, people generally dismissed the idea. Of course, those streams were virgin water for trout, with abundant fish feed. They grew undisturbed. Nobody paid any attention to them, until the third spring. At spawning time, in March and early April, the fish began going up every little branch seeking places to spawn; it was discovered that the streams were full of big rainbow trout. We had a large watering trough at the branch below the house. It was here that the wash kettles were set up for doing the family laundry. The trough was filled by gravity flow through a series of waterspouts made by nailing planks together in a V-shape. I remember so well the time mother dipped a large rainbow out of the trough when carrying water from there to the wash kettles. The trout had gone up the branch and got trapped in the waterspouts and carried down into the trough.

Dr. Randolph Shields' paternal grandmother, Aunt Jane Shields Moody (her second husband was R. M. Moody, according to Dr. Randolph's compendium of Cades Cove families heretofore referred to), owned a large white shepherd dog. On his route one morning, as the trout were making their first big spawning runs, my father noticed that dog running frantically along the branch at the rear of Aunt Jane Moody's house. Investigating, he found that the dog was excited about rainbow trout so big the water did not cover them completely—their backs were out of the water.

When the word went abroad, people came from near and far. In about 1911 I recall seeing great schools of tremendous rainbows, weaving slowly upstream across the road from the south side of our farm. But the fish population was depleted by the heavy fishing pressure on the streams, by the dynamiting and seining by people not content to use hook and line. The late John McCaulley, who was a great hunter and fisherman, told me that in the summer of 1912 he and his brother Joe fished around the Big Horseshoe of Abrams Creek one day and caught thirty-six trout, the least of which was eighteen inches long.

In the early 1930s, when my brother-in-law Charles S. Dunn was the park ranger on the Tennessee portion of Great Smoky Mountains National Park, trout rearing pools were built at the Chimneys and in the upper end of Cades Cove, all with Civilian Conservation Corps labor. Some restocking of the streams resulted from that effort. But the official policy of the National Park Service now is to give very low priority to stocking the streams, although there are over 600 miles of prime trout streams in the park.

Trout Fishing in Cades Cove

My brother Clay became an expert trout fisherman and even designed a lure that was popular among the locals.

eginning when I was old enough to fish, I caught a lot of trout in Abrams Creek and tributaries. Before my brothers were old enough to negotiate the rough waters of Abrams Creek, our

A group of Cades Cove men with a fresh catch of trout.

neighbor Virgil Burchfield was my fishing buddy. Virgil had that certain indefinable faculty of sensing the most potentially productive spots along the stream, and a finesse in presentation and manipulation of lures that marks an expert fisherman. My brother Henry Clay and I spent many happy hours fishing in those streams. He really became an expert and caught many big fish. He learned fly fishing from the late General Cary F. Spence, of Knoxville, who used to take him along to carry his creel. I treasure the moving pictures of various fishing excursions, including those showing Henry Clay landing a nice trout on Abrams Creek and scenes of me and my sons on fishing trips. In 1939 Clay designed a streamer fly which he called Oliver's Whirling Dervish, and sent his hook specifications and a colored drawing to a man in Flint, Michigan and asked him to make up three of them. Abrams Creek was closed in 1938 and 1939. On opening day of 1940, May 16, the fishing was fair but not what we expected after the stream had been closed for two years. No one had a limit. About mid-afternoon, Clay decided to try his new streamer—with a small brass spinner. The result was amazing, the way trout hit that streamer fly! Everybody wanted some of them. Henry Clay placed a rush order for six dozen more, and in the next two years he ordered and sold several more dozens, so great was the demand. The secret, I think, was the streamer's close resemblance to a minnow. A trout will always go for a minnow if it is properly presented. I still have one original of Oliver's Whirling Dervish, which I have kept for seed. A few years ago Orvis made up some of these for me, using my original as a pattern. This streamer, with a small brass or copper spinner, when worked along the stream bottom, will take more large trout than any artificial lure I have ever used. In 1935 Clay caught a thirty-five inch rainbow on the Big Horseshoe, using a minnow. During my time in high school, my brothers and I would go to Abrams Falls for two or three days when I got home from school. Memorable times, camping and fishing.

Physicians and Medical Attention

Dr. James M. Saults of Cades Cove, who died while attending the birth of my sister Johnnie Geneva.

In my lifetime the only doctor who lived in Cades Cove was Dr. James M. Saults(z). I remember him very well, a tall, angular, bald man with a long white beard flowing over his chest. He was called to our house on July 27, 1914 to attend to my mother at the birth of my sister Johnnie Geneva. There he suddenly became very ill, had to go to bed and died in a short time. Presumably, he suffered a severe heart attack.

An instance I recall when the service of a physician was dispensed with was the occasion a rather large and discolored swelling developed

Above, Clay, Burley Harmon, Geneva, Lucille and Winston. In the early 1920s, Dr. G. D. LeQuire and Dr. J. E. Carson, of Maryville, came to our house and performed tonsillectomies on my sister Lucille, me, and Burley Harmon, a neighbor child.

on the front of my right thigh just below my groin. This resulted from bracing my pitchfork handle against my thigh for leverage in throwing heavy bundles of wheat onto the wagon to transport the grain into the barn. When this swollen place became painful, my father decided it should be lanced. He got his caponizing knife to use as a lancet, sharpened and sterilized it by boiling it in water. Mother and the other children left the house. Without benefit of anesthetic or anything to assuage the pain, father cut two small holes in the swollen area, where he thought openings should be made, about two inches apart. I still bear the scars. Pus from the infection poured from both openings. With a medicine dropper he then injected hydrogen peroxide into each opening. This was an ordeal for

Dr. *G. D. LeQuire who performed the tonsillectomies.*

him and for me, but the operation was successful. Of course, he could not give me anti-tetanus shots. A couple of weeks later, before the wounds were fully healed, my cousin Clark Feezell came to visit me. He and I built a boat of sorts, carried it the five hundred yards to the creek, and paddled it up and down the creek until we were exhausted and wet. My wounds became infected and within a day I developed a temperature. Father sent for Dr. B. E. DeLozier, who then lived at Townsend. He pulled me through, although he said I would have developed tetanus in another day. In later years, Dr. DeLozier's son Hugh E. DeLozier and I were partners in the practice of law. In the early 1920s, Dr. G. D. LeQuire and Dr. J. E. Carson, of Maryville, came to our house and did a tonsillectomy on my mother, Lucille, me, and a neighbor child, Burley Harmon. These doctors set up an operating room in our house; using ether as an anesthetic, the doctors finished their work by mid-afternoon. They then walked over the ridge to the Laurel Branch entrance to Abrams Creek and went swimming in the large deep pool which all the cove boys of several generations used as a swimming hole.

I have mentioned a Dr. Jenkins of Townsend, who saved my life when I was a baby by administering diptheria antitoxin and lancing my neck. When we lived at the Fisher Place, my father was stricken on his route with what, in the light of present medical knowledge, was acute appendicitis. He could get no further than grandfather Oliver's, where he had to go to bed.

To combat a hook-worm infection, the county initiated a project to build outhouses for every home in the cove.

Dr. Jenkins and a Dr. Blankenship from Maryville were summoned, and remained with him constantly for two or three days, during which time his appendix burst. From that point he began to improve under the attention and medication of the physicians. I remember that very well.

About 1915 or 1916, Blount County's county physician, Dr. K. A. Bryant and the county nurse made a house-to-house survey in the cove and discovered widespread hook-worm infestation. Following treatment of those infected, Blount County initiated a program of building sanitary outdoor toilets for every home in the cove, upon Dr. Bryant's recommendation. I recall accompanying Dr. Bryant and the nurse on their initial rounds to show them where homes were located. The total program effectively eliminated the problem. Albert Hill was in charge of the outhouse construction.

A Fine Place for Men and Dogs

*General Washington Harmon who was a son
of Uncle Sam and Aunt Polly Harmon.*

Burley Harmon was a daughter of Uncle Sam and Aunt Polly Harmon, who lived on the Cooper Road, about two miles back in the hills from our house, where they had bought about thirty acres from Hamp Myers. I recall how the whole family worked to clear that land and establish their home. They first built a barn and lived in it until their house was finished. Aunt Polly was a midwife and was in considerable demand. Two sons, Austin and General, and daughters Retta and Braska frequently worked for us. When father wanted any of the Harmon family to work, he would send me to their house early in the morning before daylight. For a light, I carried a pine-torch, a piece of rich pine about a foot long which was lighted at

Johnny Buchanan at left, with Jake
Garland. Jake Garland shot and
killed General Harmon,
claiming self defense.

one end and carried in the hand. The Harmons were industrious and hard working people, honest and dependable. They were Mormons (Church of the Latter Day Saints). Periodically, itinerant Mormon elders visited briefly with the Harmon and Charlie Garland families.

Aunt Polly Harmon told us about an incident related by two of the traveling Mormon preachers. They said that while traveling through the mountains of western North Carolina, they saw a woman plowing corn—with a steer hitched to the plow. Engaging her in conversation, they talked at length and in glowing terms about the beauty and grandeur of the mountains. To all of which the woman simply made this significant observation: "Yes, it's a fine place for men and dogs, but it's hell on women and steers".

General Harmon was shot to death by Jake Garland during a disagreement involving money. General claimed Jake owed him wages. Only the two of them were present. At his trial Jake claimed he acted in self defense, insisting General attacked him with a rock and struck him on the head.

Of Horses, Dogs, and Bees

This is Papa riding one of our horses and our dog tagging along.

In my early teens my father bought a team of big black horses from Mr. Sherman Myers, of Townsend. They were full brothers, very gentle and manageable, named Gib and Joe. I was plowing with a turning plow when I was not strong enough to turn the heavy plow at the corners; Gib and Joe did that for me, on command. I drove that team to Townsend and back, alone, to get fertilizer, oats for horse feed, and other supplies shipped from Maryville to the Townsend depot. My mother was always apprehensive when I made those trips alone over the mountains. But Gib and Joe were so gentle and responsive that I never had any difficulty at all. I did much of the corn plowing with that team after we got a two-horse riding cultivator, as well as hay mowing and other horsepower work.

We had another horse that holds a special place in my memory. Father bought him from General L. D. Tyson of Knoxville. So, he was named

Clay is in the photo to the left and Lucille to the right, each one with a beloved dog of ours.

Tyse. A medium sized bay, father rode him on the mail route every second day. Always during high water on Forge Creek, following heavy rains, and when the fords were frozen over in winter, Tyse would face the current and ease at an angle across swollen streams, and would very cautiously paw a path through ice. In those days the fords were not bridged as they are today. Small drains across the roads were often covered with wooden bridges two or three feet wide. These boards soon became rotten and had to be replaced. Tyse ran a foot through decayed places in such little bridges so many times that no one but father could ride him across any wooden bridge, and sometimes had to touch him a bit with the spurs before he would proceed. I rode Tyse to mill the first time I ever took corn to Uncle Jim Cable's mill. Father was using our only saddle. So, using several burlap bags in lieu of a saddle, a bushel of shelled corn was evenly divided in the meal sack so as to balance it on the horse. When I got to the Abrams Creek bridge Tyse would not go across. So I had to slide off carefully to avoid dislodging my sack of corn, and lead Tyse across the bridge. Leading him close to the fence on the other side, I remounted from the top of the fence. At the mill, when I got off of Tyse the sack fell off on top of me. After hitching him, I carried my sack into the mill. Tyse was a good saddle horse, but he would not work in harness. It distressed all the family when father decided to sell him after many years of service. A few years later, a Cove family by the name of Garland acquired Tyse. They reported that he tried to stop at our house every time they passed, and tried to stop at every mail box.

Here I want to set down my memories of two extraordinary dogs. Aunt Jane Moody gave me a dark brown shepherd pup, with white throat and white front feet. We named him Jack. As he grew and developed he came to resemble and have the carriage of a wolf. He was highly intelligent and was very devoted to all the family. At maturity he was quite large. But before he was a year old he began going alone into the hills above our house to hunt squirrels. He could be heard barking when he treed one. One winter morning I heard Jack barking when I came out of the barn after feeding the cattle. Mother very reluctantly gave me permission to take the shotgun and one cartridge to go after the squirrel, but I had to agree not to load the gun until ready to shoot. I missed. In that predicament, I wrote a note on an envelope, asking mother to send my sister Lucille with some more ammunition, put the envelope under Jack's collar and told him to go home. Mother had heard my shot, and when she saw Jack with the envelope under his collar, she just knew I had shot myself. She read the note and sent Lucille with more cartridges. Jack accompanied her, and I got the squirrel. Afterwards, we had to hurry to get to school on time. Mother could not consent to letting me take the gun on trips into the foothills to check on hogs and cattle; she always seemed less apprehensive about me going alone because Jack went along. When I went fishing alone, Jack was my constant companion; he walked along on the rocks in the creek and became excited when I caught a trout.

The other dog that stands out in my memory was our son Mike's white and tan English setter named Major, given to him as a pup sired by an outstanding setter owned by an avid bird hunter friend of mine in Monroe County. By Mike's long and patient and painstaking training, Major developed into a superb bird dog—a master technician in his craft. Once Mike and a friend, who owned a setter, and I were quail hunting in Loudon County. Major found a covey, the other setter dutifully backed him. I was taking movies of the action. Instead of moving up behind the dogs, Mike and our friend moved in facing them, which caused the birds to flush back over the dogs. Major jumped high and caught a quail in full flight as they flew over the dogs. I have all of that on movie film, as well as other memorable bird hunting trips. Another dog came to us in unusual circumstances. During the influenza epidemic of 1918-1919, a magnificent yellow collie followed my father home one day in December, 1918. At the time, we had no idea who he belonged to. That dog and Jack had a definite dislike for each other. So we asked our tenant in the Elijah Oliver house at the time, Jim Hatcher and family, to keep the collie until we could find his owner. Then came hog killing time; Jim Hatcher was helping, as were Jesse Burchfield and son Virgil. The smell of blood associated with the operation made the dogs' mutual antipathy more acute. When Virgil and I finished lunch, the dogs were sitting on opposite ends of our long front porch glowering at each other. Never before or since did I ever witness such a dog fight. I became scared that one would kill the other, so ferociously were they fighting, and I decided to try to separate them and stepped between them. I still bear a scar on each side of my right leg just below my knee where one of the dogs bit me through and through. By that time my father and the other men ran out and got them apart by throwing a bucket of cold water on them.

Father later learned the collie belonged to the family of William Tyre (Billie) Shields, who, with two of the children, died of influenza about the

Papa wasn't the only one who raised bees. Here is my Uncle Henry Whitehead with bees and a smoker, which was used to quiet the bees.

time the collie fell in behind my father somewhere on his route and followed him home. After the death of Billie Shields and the two children, his widow, whose maiden name was Emily Jane Roberts, moved with the other children to a house built for them on her parents' farm in the upper end of Cades Cove. Her parents were Samuel and Martha Jane Roberts. Emily's new house, built by her brother, J. Witt Roberts, was located in the area of the present Park Service campground. One Sunday in the spring of 1919, I took the collie home. The reunion of the dog and the children was indeed something to see.

My first experience with bees, aside from watching them at swarming time—already noted, was helping my father "rob" (harvest the honey) at grandfather Whitehead's. I operated the bee smoker to keep the bees under control as much as possible. We carried the supers of honey to the kitchen

Some beekeepers in the Smokies used a more rustic way of beekeeping. This bee gum is made from naturally hollowed black gum tree logs. Black gum trees tend to rot from the inside out, making a convenient place to grow a hive of bees. The beekeeper places cross-sticks inside the stump for the bees to build their honeycomb around, a few notches along the bottom for ingress and egress, and a lid is all you need.

(Matilda's log house) where she and my mother cut the comb honey from the frames and packed it in tin pails. This in itself was a hazardous operation because there were no screens on the windows to keep out the bees attracted to the honey processing. I have mentioned the 100 foot bee shed my father built to house the bees acquired from grandfather Whitehead. It included a platform made of pine two-by-fours, suspended about eighteen inches from the ground by heavy galvanized wire anchored to the rafters along the entire front side of the shed. The purpose of that suspended platform, on which the hives were placed eight or ten inches apart, was to prevent ants from reaching and entering the hives.

As long as I remained at home I worked with the bees, assisting with whatever was to be done—assembling frames and installing foundation combs, making some of the brood boxes and supers from specially sawed white pine boards, hiving swarms, etc. In swarming season (early spring and summer), when a swarm came out mother would call me from the field to come and get the swarm into a hive. The bees usually settled in an apple tree nearby, which was accessible by a ladder. A brood chamber, with foundation filled frames in place, was positioned on a table under the swarm. The limb on which the bees were settled was gently cut off and carried down the ladder and placed on the table in front of the hive, which they would enter promptly and take up their habitation in the new home. Of course, it is always prudent to exercise reasonable caution with bees. I always wore a bee veil and gloves and tied the bottoms of my overall legs when hiving a swarm of bees, just in case part of the mass came loose and fell to the ground in the process of getting them out of the tree. When that occurs, as it did on occasion, the bees that fall will arise immediately and angrily attack.

Bees can be very dangerous. In hot weather a large mass of them will come out of the hive and spread out all over the front end of it. Once two geese walked under such a hive and rubbed a lot of bees off onto themselves, and were stung to death. The same thing happened to a lamb.

One hot day I began plowing corn with a riding cultivator in the field adjacent to the bee shed. Many bees were in the air, going from and returning to the hives; it was during a heavy tulip poplar honey flow. The bees began to sting Gib and Joe when I got to the end of the field nearest the bee shed. The horses began trying to lay down, their instinct being to roll on the ground to rub off the bees; if that had occurred they would have been stung to death. But I layed on the whip and kept them going at a run until we got out of the field, avoiding disaster.

Apples and Chestnuts

Apple peeling time was an occasion for work as well as socializing.

hen my father bought the Fisher Place, he set out quite a number of apple trees, including various varieties. In those days, spraying fruit trees was an unheard of procedure; nor was it necessary, because there were no insects or diseases to contend with. Pruning was the only care required. My sister Lucile and I had the annual chore of returning to the Fisher Place to harvest the apples and carry them across the road and store them in the barn loft.

Among other apple varieties, grandfather Oliver had quite a number of Winter John trees. Some called them Sour Johns. Although they were sour, those medium-sized white to yellowish apples were very juicy and especially good for making jelly and apple butter, and were a cash crop for that reason. In the fall, people hauled these apples to Maryville where they were always in great demand.

My parents permitted me to accompany grandfather Oliver on such a trip in November, 1918. He carried sufficient feed for the mules, and a "grub box" grandmother filled with a variety of provisions for us. We started from the Cove on November 10, camped that night at a waggoners' campground near Maryville, and drove on to Rockford the next morning and peddled apples in that community. When the afternoon Knoxville newspaper arrived, large headlines proclaimed the signing of the Armistice that morning, ending World War I. Church bells rang, factory whistles blew, everyone exultant that the war was over, and triumphantly for the Allies.

During the afternoon, we chanced to meet up with Mr. Theodore Caldwell, who owned a large farm at Rockford, and who had bought cattle from us and others in Cades Cove. He insisted that we spend the night at his home. I have always remembered the gracious hospitality of Mr. Caldwell and his family, and Armistice Day 1918. The next morning, we drove into Maryville, parked the wagon and team on Cusick Street where we sold the remainder of our load of apples in a short time, and started the two-day trip back to the Cove. For an eleven year old, this was a memorable experience.

George Powell, who lived in the Chestnut Flats area of the Cove, to whom I shall refer later, had a large apple orchard. Varieties included the Mountain Boomer—a large yellow apple, and the Black Ben Davis—a large apple of such deep red color it was almost black. For a number of years, my father sent a collection of both varieties as exhibits to the annual fair in Knoxville.

The mountains were practically covered with chestnut trees in many areas. Before those trees were all killed by a fungus commonly referred to as the chestnut blight, the annual yield of chestnuts was immense, immeasurable. Hogs ranged on the mountain during the fall of the year really got fat on the chestnuts. I recall the memorable occasions when a group of teenagers, accompanied by two or three couples of parents, would make an overnight trip to the Rye Patch cabin to get chestnuts; in a few hours we could pick up as many as we were able to carry home. One of the outlying communities was called Chestnut Flats; I used to accompany my father as he carried the mail to that area, and he would leave me there to pick up chestnuts until late afternoon.

The first chestnut trip to Smoky Mountain that I remember, however, was when I was about three years old. My parents took grandfather and grandmother Oliver to the first cabin described above for a week's vacation. It was in the fall when chestnuts were falling. Besides the chestnuts, I also distinctly recall being stung by yellow jackets whose nest, unknown to me, was in a nearby hollow stump which my curiosity prompted me to explore.

Photograph by Maryann Kressig

Food had to be canned, pickled, dried, smoked, stored in the root cellar, or preserved in various ways to make sure we had enough to get through the winter.

ontrary to what some misinformed and uninformed persons may have believed and written, the people of Cades Cove, for the most part, lived well. They produced a great variety of food, their own beef and lamb, and pork and poultry, and milk and butter; they grew corn for meal and hominy and feed; their wheat was hauled to Miller Will Lawson's mill at Townsend or to the Peery Brothers' mill at Walland, and either made into flour or exchanged for flour the miller had on hand. Winter found, in most households, an adequate supply of canned food—vegetables, fruits, and assorted berries (blackberries, huckleberries or blueberries), honey, jellies and jams, and apple butter and preserves. There was always kraut and pickled

The Walker sisters, who lived in nearby Greenbrier Cove, carding and spinning wool. Many mountain folk raised sheep for wool. The raw wool had to be washed, carded,—which aligns all the tufts in one direction—, spun into yarn, and woven into fabric. Then the task of making clothes began. Small wonder that when bolts of fabric became widely available people abandoned the old ways and bought their cloth from catalogs and stores.

beans and dried apples and leather britches beans. Without a storage cellar, sweet potatoes, Irish potatoes, turnips and cabbage were buried, "holed up," in the garden to preserve them during the winter. In that process a thick layer of straw was placed on the ground in a round shape; cabbage or turnips or potatoes were stacked layer on layer in a cone-like arrangement, tapering to the top; this mound was completely covered with straw, and was then over laid with soil to protect the straw and seal the mound. A small trench was made around the base to keep water out. To remove an item it was only necessary to make a small opening in the side of the mound, and then reseal it.

To make leather britches beans, green beans are prepared ready for cooking but left unbroken and then are strung on a strong double thread, using a large needle, and hung up to dry. Soaked over-night and cooked with a piece of ham hock, leather britches beans are really delicious.

Leather britches hung on the porch to dry.

Mother had Jordan Wilcox make her two barrels of about thirty-gallon capacity, one used for sauerkraut and the other for pickled beans. Making the annual supply of kraut and pickled beans was quite a chore, but both were enjoyable in winter.

The sheep were sheared in the spring before going to the mountain for the summer. We shipped most of the wool to market, but mother always retained enough for home use. This she washed several times to eliminate the natural oils and the characteristic odor. She would form the wool into rolls with two-handled rectangular boards thickly studded on one side with tiny, stiff steel wires. These steel brushes were called cards, the purpose of which was to prepare the wool for spinning. The carded rolls were spun into thread on the spinning wheel. With this wool thread, mother knitted our winter socks and stockings, which were dyed when finished. Many were the hours she spent in the washing, carding, spinning and knitting process. But as I observed her as she employed these skills, and others, perfected by experience, it always seemed to me that she really enjoyed providing comforts and necessities for her family. Her's was truly a labor of love.

This is the Southern Methodist Church.

our churches were in Cades Cove: The Primitive Baptist, the Northern Methodist, the Southern Methodist, and the Missionary Baptist. As noted above, my great-great grandfather John Oliver was one of the organizers of the Primitive Baptist Church, and great grandfather Oliver was an active member for many years. My father was ordained as a minister in that church on May 21, 1916, having been a member since February 1894.

This is the Primitive Baptist Church, where I attended as a child.

Mother became a member in February, 1906. Lucile, Winston, and I were members. I recall very distinctly the day Lucile and I were baptized. It was a very cold winter day and mush ice was floating in the water. The place

This is the Missionary Baptist Church.

This was the baptizing of my brother Winston.

was in Abrams Creek near Uncle Noah Burchfield's house. There was a pool about waist deep just above Uncle Noah's footlog. He invited those who were to be baptized to change clothes in his house. The first time I remember going to church was at the Primitive Baptist Church. My sister Lucile and I sat on a tanned sheep skin placed on the floor in the rear of the buggy. In those days, people rode horses and drove wagons and buggies to church.

The Southern Methodist church (on the north side of the Cove) is the first one on the right side of the loop road—a building with two front doors. It was built by Preacher John McCampbell, a Methodist preacher-school teacher-carpenter who lived in Tuckaleechee Cove. His wife was a daughter of Dr. J. M. Saults(z). Preacher McCampbell took a contract to build this church in 100 days for $100.00. This church flourished for many years, evident by the large number buried in that cemetery.

The Northern Methodist church (on the south side of the cove) was located on a hill on the right side of the loop road, a few hundred yards east of the Kermit Caughron bee yard. I remember that church very well.

The last time I was there was at the funeral of Gular Harmon, who was the father of Sam Harmon and lived with the Harmon family in his declining years. Squire Daniel B. Lawson was one of the moving spirits in the establishing of this church, contributing the land and the building materials. It was named Hopewell Methodist Church. Because of lack of care, the building gradually deteriorated to the point that it fell into ruins and was removed by the Park Service. However, the Park Service has responsibility for care of the cemetery.

The Missionary Baptist church is a short distance west of the Southern Methodist church, and is located at the intersection of the loop road and the one-way trans-mountain road to Townsend. The original church was located on Hyatt Lane. Standing on a small hill, it could be seen from one end of the cove to the other. I remember it very well. Dr. Randolph Shields records in his book about the Cades Cove families that Dr. J. M. (James Marian) Saults(z) was also a minister and served a few years as pastor of the Missionary Baptist Church while it was located on Hyatt Lane.

The Schools of Cades Cove

Cades Cove School group with Elmer Shields as teacher, 1921.

The first school I attended was the one room grade school in the lower end of the Cove. It was located on the loop road about one hundred yards north of the first store and home of Uncle Russ and Aunt Jane Burchfield mentioned above. George D. Roberts was the teacher. In 1916 a new consolidated school began operation. It was located on the left at the curve of the road leading from the loop road to the Primitive Baptist Church. This school replaced the one room schools. It was a two-story building, with a large concreted basement. On the top floor was an auditorium large enough for a basketball court, a library room and one classroom. Three classrooms occupied the first floor. The basement was never utilized for the boiler and central heating system originally envisioned. Instead, the class rooms were heated by wood burning heaters. Water was piped in a two-inch pipe line from a spring high on the side of the mountain on

Uncle Witt Shields' property. Three teachers were assigned. Those for the first term were William E. Roberts, principal, and Misses Sue Tedford and Dorothy Wells of Maryville. Mr. Roberts lived at home; and Miss Tedford and Miss Wells boarded with Mr. and Mrs. Albert Hill, whose home was at the intersection of the loop road and the Primitive Baptist Church road, as did succeeding teachers who did not live in the cove.

The terms were from July 1 to Christmas. To end the term, there was a big Christmas party in the auditorium. The boys brought in a large cedar and set it up on the stage, and helped the girls and teachers with the decoration. Some of the students brought popped popcorn from home, which was strung on thread to decorate the tree, along with tinsel and other decorations provided by the teachers. Of course, we had no electricity, and candles and kerosene lamps placed along the walls provided light and added to the festive atmosphere. Many of the parents and others came to these programs. Santa Claus always put in a timely appearance and distributed to the children the presents placed on and under the tree. The children sang traditional Christmas carols and some recited poems and readings, which had been practiced long and patiently. There was also some group singing. I attended this school through the seventh grade.

Often on Friday afternoon we would have a spelling bee. All the seats in one classroom were arranged in two parallel rows on opposite sides of the room. Two students were selected to choose up sides, which were designated as No. 1 and No. 2, and included all the students. A teacher pronounced the words, starting at one end of one side and moving to the other end, then crossing over to the other side and going to the end of it—and then crossing over to the beginning point and starting the same round again. Every word was repeated until it was spelled. The student spelling a word missed by others was moved ahead in the line to the point where the word was first missed. This was called "turning down," or moving ahead of the person or persons who missed the word. When, by this process, a student

Lower Cades Cove School group, 1916.

reached the head of the line, and successfully spelled the next word, he or she crossed over to the other side, and in doing so called out his or her side number, i.e., "Side Number 1," or "Side Number 2." This crossover was a "talley." One student was the tallier, recording on the blackboard when a student achieved a crossover. Of course, at the end of the session the side with the largest talley score was the winner. In those days, we learned the alphabet with all the sounds of the letters and were taught spelling by the phonetic method.

I remember particularly some of the principals who taught during my years in that school. There was Miss Gertrude Lawson and Mr. L. W. Bogart and Mr. S. L. Shirley, of Maryville; William E. Roberts, George H. (Little George) Myers, and John Elmer Shields, all Cades Cove men. The other teachers serving with John Elmer Shields were Misses Belle and Jessie Williams, sisters. Later John Elmer married Belle, and his brother Jack Shields married Jessie.

About the mid-1920s the school was remodeled and the second story was removed, and the building was demolished a few years later. In 1926 a one-room school was built near the Cable cemetery in the lower end of the cove to accommodate the declining school population. That school, the last one in Cades Cove, closed in 1944.

At one time, in the early 1920s I believe, a one-room school was built about a mile up the Parson Branch road from its beginning. It was called the Flint Hill School. Miss Sarah Lou Roylston, of Maryville, taught there in the 1922 and 1923 terms. She boarded with the Taylor Whitehead family whose home was on the hill just to the right side of the entrance of Parson Branch Road. In later years, Mr. and Mrs. William H. Myers (Willie and Hattie) lived in the Taylor Whitehead house for a few years, where they established a wide reputation providing meals and lodging for tourists.

As I now recall, it was during the tenure of Miss Gertrude Lawson that Henry Gregory (1906-1966) and I volunteered to get the baseball field in shape for playing. We walked to our house, hitched Gib and Joe to the wagon, loaded our turning plow and disk harrow and drove back to school and plowed and disked the baseball field. Henry and I decided to try to obtain some baseball equipment. From a Sears and Roebuck catalog we selected a couple of bats, catcher's mask and glove, half a dozen fielder's gloves and a couple of balls. Thus arriving at the total cost of these minimum needs, several of the boys agreed to contribute an equal share. We were really elated when our equipment arrived. Henry was a catcher and assumed responsibility for caring for it. At the noon hour, two people would choose up sides to form two teams. To do this, the choosers would alternate in gripping a bat hand over hand from bottom to top. The one whose hand gripped the top of the bat in that manner got to select the first player for his side. They then took time in choosing players until two teams were selected. Only a few minutes were required to complete this process. Our games lasted until the teacher's bell rang for "books." Other recess and lunch hour diversions were jumping the rope and tug-of-war. In those activities our "rope" was a wild grapevine obtained from the surrounding

The new Cades Cove Consolidated School, which opened in 1916, was much bigger and allowed us to have a gymnasium and a library.

woods. Henry Gregory was elected in his later years as a member of the Quarterly County Court of Blount County.

Wild Turkey Dinner for the Teachers

During the fall of 1916, the first year of our new Consolidated School, when my father got home from his route about 3:00 p.m. one day, he put a pair of half soles on his shoes and then asked me if I would like to go squirrel hunting. How well do I remember that! We went up the hollow where the Elijah Oliver springhouse is located. Stopping to rest at the top of the ridge, a noise which I could not identify was audible in the distance. Father said it was squirrels, and disappeared in that direction to investigate, cautioning me to remain where I was until he returned. After a short while I heard the report of his 16 gauge single barrel Remington shotgun, which was followed by what seemed to be some kind of commotion overhead through the trees. He had found some wild turkeys flying up in the trees to roost, which accounted for the first noise we heard. Approaching carefully, he sighted two turkeys sitting side by side on a limb and killed both of them, a gobbler and a hen, at one shot. The noises I then heard was the others flying away through the trees. That gobbler was a heavy load for me to carry home. My mother decided this was the time to invite the teachers, Misses Wells and Tedford, to spend a night with us. It was a custom for teachers to visit with patrons during the school year. So mother told us to ask these two teachers to come home with us the next day. She had prepared one of those turkeys, with her consummate skill, complete with gravy and dressing, and loaded the table with the usual fresh vegetables, cornbread and biscuits.

This was a dinner to remember, and I am sure Miss Wells and Miss Tedford never forgot that visit to our house.

Errands to Maryville

On a trip to Maryville to sell produce.

everal times in my youth, father sent me to Maryville on various errands. It was necessary on those occasions to get up in time to start by 3:00 a.m. I walked to the Riverside station, about where Wilson's Restaurant is now located, to catch the Little River Lumber Company train there at eight o'clock. By taking all the shortcuts, the total walking distance was about twelve miles. I would leave Maryville on the 3:00 p.m. train, get off at Riverside and walk home by the same route. On one of those trips I met Mr. John Hitch at the Maryville depot while waiting for the afternoon train. When I introduced myself, he at once remembered that father bought Ol' Black Joe from him. He insisted that I go home with him for the night. We got off the train at Hubbard station and walked to the Hitch home, a large brick house now included in the Lambert Acres Golf Course. There I met all the Hitch children, all of whom became good friends of my own family in later years. Mr. Hitch took me through his barns and showed me his herd of Black Aberdeen Angus cattle. He put me back on the train at Hubbard station the next morning. My parents were not apprehensive when I did not come home the previous night. They concluded I had spent that night with some of our relatives. When I told them about Mr. Hitch taking me home with him they were very appreciative of his kindness and hospitality.

A Trip With Mother

*Jack and Nancy Tipton, one of the families
we stayed with on our trip.*

In May of 1920, my mother took her children (Lucile, Geneva, Henry Clay, Winston, and me) to visit the families of Uncle Lee Feezell and Uncle Preston Roberts. Uncle Lee married Mary Jane Oliver, and Uncle Preston married Martha Angeline Oliver, my father's sisters. I fix the date from Winston's age at that time; he was born on August 30, 1919, and was still wearing a long dress when we made that trip. We rode to Townsend with Uncle Jim Cable in his wagon. It was one of his trips to haul merchandise to Uncle Russ Burchfield's store. We spent the first night with the Jack Tipton family at Townsend. Next morning we got on the Little River Lumber Company train to Walland; there we had to change to the Southern Railway train to Maryville. From the Maryville depot we walked across town to the Louisville and Nashville Railway depot, where we got an L & N train to Binfield. Uncle Lee and his son Clark met us there. After staying a few days with them, we went back to Maryville on the L & N. In Maryville mother took us to the Eugene Webb studio for a group photo. She was holding Winston in her lap, in his long white dress, and the rest of us were arranged around her. Then we got on the Southern train at the Maryville depot, got off at Amerine Station, and walked the half mile to Uncle Preston's house. After a couple of days there, we got back on the train at Amerine Station and went to Townsend, changing to the Little River Lumber Company

These are the children of Jack and Nancy Tipton: Hoyt, Jeff, Floyd, Noah, and Ocie.

train at Walland. Again we spent a night with the Jack Tipton family. In the meantime Jack Tipton's mother, Cansada (Kans) Tipton, had come for a visit with them. She was a deaf mute. The next morning she told Jack's family, who could communicate with her, that her head was roaring and this meant impending bad news. Uncle Monroe LeQuire was the "Star Route" mail carrier, transporting mail between the Townsend and Cades Cove post offices. When he arrived at Townsend that morning, he brought the news that the preceding day a tombstone had fallen on little Lora Gregory, a grandaughter of Aunt Kans and Uncle Isaac (Ike) Tipton. Their daughter Naomi Tipton Gregory, who married John C. Gregory, and another lady had gone to the cemetery to remove weeds and rubbish from some graves. Playing around meanwhile, this child apparently came in contact with a large tombstone which had become unsteady on

Monroe and Bett LeQuire and family. Standing in the back are John, Martha, Ida, Joe, and Fred. In the front are Monroe and Bett and a foster child named Mayme Sawyer.

its base, and it toppled over on her. In the stress of the moment, the child's mother lifted the stone off of her. It was said the weight of the stone would have taxed the strength of two men. Undoubtedly due to her mother's quick action, Lora suffered no permanent injury.

We returned home the same way we went to Townsend, in the wagon of Uncle Jim Cable, who came to the Townsend depot for supplies for Uncle Russ Burchfield's store. For mother and us children this trip was a happy and memorable experience. On that trip I acquired two Belgian Hare rabbits from cousins Floyd and James Roberts. As it turned out, I had two females instead of a pair. Sam Tipton, who was helping with construction of our new barn that summer, informed me his daughter Nancy (Mrs. Willie E. Wright) had some rabbits of the same breed. She loaned me one of her males for a few weeks. Within a short time I had so many rabbits that the lot I had built would no longer hold them and I had to turn them loose to roam at will.

Memories of Uncle Russell D. Burchfield and Aunt Jane

Uncle Russell Burchfield (82 years old) and wife Aunt Jane (83 years old).

n his research, Dr. Randolph Shields learned that Dr. Saults(z) built a home and store building on the right of the loop road "just before the turn into the Cable Mill area," bought the merchandise which Dan and Becky Cable had in their store, and set his son Riley Saults(z) up in the general store business; and that Riley sold to Henry Hawkins in 1902.

A few years later, that home and store building were acquired by Uncle Russ Burchfield and Aunt Jane. They lived there and operated a store until 1920, when they built a new home and new store building about a mile straight ahead from the Cable Mill intersection. After Uncle Russ's death in 1925, Aunt Jane continued with the store until the early 1930s. It was customary for people to take eggs and chickens to the store to pay for their

This was the building that housed Uncle Noah and Aunt Jane's store.

merchandise. They were paid the going prices. Periodically, the eggs were crated in egg cases, the chickens were put in coops, and shipped to produce dealers in Knoxville. Uncle Jim Cable hauled the chickens and eggs to the Townsend depot, and brought back any ordered merchandise that had arrived there. In winter Uncle Russ also bought fur pelts (coon, possum, mink, muskrat, skunk), which he in turn sold to Jerry Hearon—who lived in Happy Valley and made frequent trips to the Cove in winter to buy fur. On those trips Jerry stayed with Uncle Russ and Aunt Jane, and always took time to catch them a mess of trout from Abrams Creek. He always carried a hook and line around his hat band, and for a fishing rod he would cut a suitable small slender maple when he reached the stream. He dug a Prince Albert tobacco can of worms for bait and he never failed to catch fish. Once he took me along, and gave me six rainbows that were eighteen inches long.

As a youngster I often helped crate eggs for shipment. Aunt Jane cooked those that froze in winter. In the store they stocked hardware items such as axes, hoes, horse collars and hames, horse and mule shoes, chains, assorted nails and horseshoe nails; shoes in assorted sizes and styles for men, women and children; men's work shirts and overalls; a variety of cloth "piece goods" in bolts, including a striped cloth called "hickory" which was widely used to make shirts for men and boys; and oil cloth, used for table covers. Coffee (green coffee beans) came in cotton-lined burlap bags, as did sugar, all of which was sold by the pound. The green coffee had to be roasted by the customer and ground in a small coffee mill—ours was attached to the wall in the kitchen. Pure hog lard, and also a substitute product made from cotton seed, came in large tin cans, and was likewise measured out and sold by the pound. Shotgun and rifle ammunition was also available; and Uncle Russ would break a box and sell fewer cartridges if the customer didn't have the price of an entire box. And there was apple and mule chewing tobacco, snuff, Prince Albert and Bull Durham smoking tobacco, epsom salts, castor oil, black draught, liniments for man and beast (including Japanese Oil—a wonderful medicine for colic for humans and animals which apparently has disappeared from the market), various other nonprescription patent medicines, and assorted chewing gum and candies.

I recall that traveling salesmen, called "drummers," visited the Cove merchants from time to time and took their orders for desired items of merchandise, which was later shipped to the Townsend depot where upon notice, the merchants picked up their goods. One drummer I recall was Robert Gregg. I distinctly remember when he spent a night at our house. He had a large buggy pulled by two beautiful bay horses, wore a derby and was very well dressed. It was shortly after Christmas, and he gave us some raisins which had been processed in bunches—stems and all. We children had not tasted raisins before. This, with some fancy candy, was really a great treat for all of us. I never saw Robert Gregg before or since. In her book *Whitehead and Related Families*, Mrs. Fred Rhyne (Margaret Whitehead) records that Robert Gregg, (salesman and drummer), lived at Friendsville, Tennessee and was a son of Monroe and Elizabeth Whitehead Gregg.

Each year Uncle Russ and Aunt Jane made a trip to Knoxville to buy

Occasionally a local drummer would roll through the Cove and supply goods to the store as well as individuals.

merchandise from wholesale houses to replenish their store stock. Once they took me along. This was a memorable event indeed. We went to Townsend in their buggy, spent the night with his brother-in-law Jack Tipton and family. We rode the train to Knoxville in the morning. I do not remember the name of the hotel where we stayed in Knoxville. Early the first morning there, a red fire engine, pulled by four magnificent white horses, came roaring down the street. The men in their firefighting gear, the bell ringing and the horses at full gallop, was a sight I shall never forget. After two or three days of shopping, we went back to Townsend on the train, and returned in the buggy to the cove.

Uncle Russ helped me take salt to the herders' cabin on two or three occasions, for our cattle and sheep on the range. We rode horses and took two hundred pounds of salt about May. On one such trip, when Joe McCaulley and Jack Godfrey were the herders, we arrived about noon. Jack Godfrey had killed a turkey gobbler that morning. Joe made biscuits and fried slices of turkey breast for our lunch. Some meals stand out in one's memory; that lunch is a treasured memory.

In the early 1920s, when Ol' Black Joe had lived out his usefulness as a herd sire, Uncle Russ and I drove him and some other cattle through the Chilhowee Mountains along the Cooper Road, to Maryville. We got to the home of his brother, Charlie Burchfield, near Maryville, the first day. The next morning we drove the cattle into Maryville, down Court Street past the Court House, and to Harper's stock scales located about where the Broadway United Methodist Church now stands—where they were sold.

Coffee (green coffee beans) came in cotton-lined burlap bags, as did sugar, all of which was sold by the pound. The green coffee had to be roasted by the customer and ground in a small coffee mill.

Aunt Becky Cable—
A Legend in Her Own Time

Aunt Becky Cable was truly a legendary figure in the Cove. She raised her brother Dan's children when he and his wife became incapacitated; she tended her farm without help, doing all the work of a man and a woman to keep the little farm going; and she gained the admiration of most in Cades Cove as a hard working mountain woman who never wasted a minute.

Rebecca Ann (Aunt Becky) Cable, 1844–1940, lived her entire life in Cades Cove and was known and loved by everyone in the community. She was a sister of James V. Cable (Uncle Jim—the miller) and Daniel

The challenge of raising her brother's children was doubly hard because Effie was severely retarded and Perry never learned to speak.

Cable. Their parents were John Primer Cable and Elizabeth Whitehead Cable. Having never married, Aunt Becky made her home with the family of her brother Dan who married Alice White. Dan and Alice had four children, viz., Ethel Effie, Mary Jane, James Perry, and Benjamin Leonard. Effie was severely retarded, and Perry was an imbecile who never talked nor shaved and wore a long dress all his life. Dan Cable became ill after the birth of their youngest child, Benjamin Leonard, and was hospitalized in an institution. All the children were small. Their mother was in delicate health and at times was unable to care for them properly or do the housework. In those circumstances, Aunt Becky had to assume a very large measure of the responsibility of rearing the children and looking after the home and the farming operations. She worked in the fields like a man, doing whatever had to be done on the farm. I remember seeing her plowing corn in the large field adjacent to the Cable Cemetery, using a double shovel plow

Aunt Becky's house and farm were preserved by the National Park Service when the land was purchased for the park.

pulled by a mule; she worked in the hay fields and in harvesting the crops, and caring for the livestock. Janie (Mary Jane) and Len (Benjamin Leonard) were taught early to work, as were all the cove children, and they became increasingly helpful as they grew up.

Aunt Becky owned a tract of mountain land located in a wide valley high on the headwaters of Mill Creek, which had been part of her father's landholdings. In the summers, she always ranged her cattle and sheep on that tract, which was known as the Sugar Cove, so named because maple sugar and syrup were made there from the sap of the abundant sugar maple trees in that locality in the early days of the community. After Becky acquired this property it was called "Becky's Sugar Cove." She walked the several miles to this area a number of times each summer to look after her livestock. As long as she was able to work outside, she preferred to go barefooted in summer. Because of the primitive road and the nature of the terrain, she always carried her shoes on her trips to the Sugar Cove and put them on when the going got too rough for bare feet.

Converting the wool from her sheep into wool thread or "yarn," Aunt Becky did a lot of knitting. I remember the extra long wool socks and

Janie Cable married Dan Lawson.

gloves she made for my father. He had to have gloves with fingers for handling mail on his route in winter, and the long socks helped to keep his legs and feet warm as he rode horseback in winter weather. She knitted socks and stockings for her family, and for others who employed her knitting skill.

John McCaulley related that Aunt Becky called to him one day as he was passing and asked him to make her coffin and gave him a pair of long wool socks. She died on December 19, 1940, a few days past her ninety-sixth birthday, and was buried in the Cable Cemetery in the coffin John made for her. Having learned the trade from his father, John McCaulley made many coffins for deceased cove people in his lifetime.

The Becky Cable house was located on the bank of Mill Creek, on the right side of the road at the first bridge straight ahead from the Cable Mill intersection. As reported in his book *The Families of Cades Cove*, Dr. Randolph Shields ascertained that Aunt Becky and her brother Dan bought the property from Leason Gregg, who had bought it from their father and was operating a general store there; and that Becky and Dan continued the store for some eight years and then sold the stock of goods to Dr. J. M. Saults(z).

As I remember the Becky Cable house, a large kitchen and dining wing was on the rear side. When the Park Service moved the house to its present location a few yards from the Cable mill, the rear wing was not included. The smoke house and other accessory outbuildings are much as they were at the original location.

Before the present Mill Creek bridge was built, there was only a footbridge, about three feet wide, for pedestrian use. Perry Cable often sat on the end of this narrow bridge, usually bemusing himself by twirling a small stick or a string or piece of tin or cloth. It was noised about that on occasion, for no apparent reason, he would suddenly become violent. Because of that alleged propensity and his somewhat frightening looks and demeanor, I was always afraid to disturb him by using the footbridge when he was sitting on it, and many times I waded the creek to avoid him.

As Janie Cable grew up, she acquired a fine bay horse and a new rubber-tired buggy. I can see her now as she came up the road, her horse at full trot, going to the post office or on some other errand. She became expert at "piecing" quilts—sewing together by hand pieces of different colors of cloth to form various designs to use as the quilt tops. I last saw her in 1961 when I visited her at her home near Maryville in company with Mr. Justice William O. Douglas of the United States Supreme Court while he was here gathering material for an article about Cades Cove which appeared in *National Geographic* magazine in July 1962. She was then a chair-bound invalid afflicted by rheumatoid arthritis. But she was still quilting. Justice Douglas, impressed with the beauty and quality of her work, bought several of her quilts.

Another Sugar Cove

William "Will Gull" Tipton and Janie Burchfield Tipton with their children. The family lived in the Sugar Cove for a while.

nother area where the sap of sugar maple trees was used to make maple syrup and sugar is known as the Tipton Sugar Cove. Also a wide mountain valley, it is located under Gregory Bald, in a manner of speaking, and southwest of the headwaters of Forge Creek, some five or six miles above the convergence of that stream and Ekaneetlee Creek. Dr. Randolph Shields records that (Will Gull) (William Abraham) Tipton and family once lived there, as did one of his sons—(John Gull) Jonathan Absolom Tipton and family. I remember well when (John Gull) Tipton and family lived there, and also when they later moved into the Wade Myers house (just over the hill from grandfather Henry Whitehead's place) after Wade and his wife, (Matt) Martha Wilson Myers, left the Cove and relocated near Maryville following acquisition of their property for the park. Also, I recall

*Johnathan Absolom "John Gull" Tipton, "Will Gull's" son,
lived in Sugar Cove with his family as well.*

when Reverend Johnnie (Jonathan Caswell) Tipton and his family lived in the Tipton Sugar Cove for a number of years. Johnnie and his wife, Louisa Myers Tipton (a daughter of Uncle Cass and Aunt Sis Myers), raised nine of their twelve children to maturity. He became a minister in his later years. Also, one son, Roy, became a minister.

It goes without saying that the people who lived in the Tipton Sugar Cove, remote and isolated as it was, were well acquainted with hardships and the rigors of toilsome living, but nevertheless, enjoyed a large measure of happiness often denied to many in better circumstances. In the history of this country, greatness of character has often emerged from such crucibles.

Cades Cove Men
Who Made a High Mark

*I*n that connection, I often think of a number of outstanding men who came out of Cades Cove. There was William E. Roberts (referred to elsewhere); following service in World War I in France, he held a responsible position with the Aluminum Company of America for many years. His brother, George D. Roberts, who was my first school teacher, became an attorney, and served as County Court Clerk of Blount County for several years, and was then elected and reelected over and over as county judge of this county.

Dr. A. Randolph Shields

Dr. G. D. LeQuire, referred to earlier, set for himself the goal of becoming a medical doctor and surgeon, and became a most proficient and highly respected member of the medical profession. Two of his sons followed him in the healing arts. Dr. Virgil LeQuire has long been a distinguished member

John Elmer Shields

of the staff at Vanderbilt Medical School. Dr. Chester Brickey LeQuire became an exceptionally skilled physician and surgeon.

George Henry (Little George) Myers and John Elmer Shields taught at the Consolidated School, at different times, both as principals, as later noted. It must be said that both were well qualified as teachers and school administrators. John Elmer later was a successful business man in Maryville.

Dr. A. Randolph Shields, whose book about the families of Cades Cove I have consulted in these memoirs, rose from humble circumstances in early life to receive a B.A. degree from Maryville College, an M.S. and Ph. D. at the University of Tennessee, and to become professor of biology at Maryville College and chairman of that department. His brother Rodney, after employment for a time with the Aluminum Company of America, became personnel director for Kaiser Aluminum Company.

George Henry Myers

Henry Gregory's public service as a member of the Quarterly County Court of Blount Count was notable. His cousin Labe Gregory made a name for himself in high school and college

Henry Clay and Winston Oliver, my brothers.

football, and became a very successful teacher and coach at Vonore High School after graduation at Tennessee Wesleyan College.

My brother, Henry Clay Oliver, graduated from Harrison-Chilhowee Institute at Seymour, and attended the University of Tennessee. When mobilization started for World War II, Clay volunteered. He became an officer in the 82nd Airborne Division of the parachute infantry after completion of his training at Fort Benning, Georgia. Then a Captain, he and his company parachuted into battle in the North African campaign. After losing his right eye, Clay was returned to the States, where he was hospitalized and fitted with an artificial eye, and later served as an instructor at the parachute infantry school at Fort Benning. After discharge, he returned to his former employment with the Patent Button Company in Knoxville. In 1955 he accepted a position with the Fulton Syphon Division of Robertshaw Controls Com-

James R. Oliver and his father, William M. Oliver.

pany at Knoxville, where he became purchasing agent, and in 1957 was named General Superintendent.

My brother Hugh R. Oliver was a Thunderbolt (fighter) pilot in the Air Force, in the European Theatre, in World War II. Thereafter, he served with distinction in various Air Force assignments. Following separation from the service, he graduated from the University of Tennessee Law School, was admitted to the bar, and after practicing law a couple of years in Maryville was recalled to active duty. This tour of duty took him to Korea and several other places. He then decided to stay in the Air Force, in which he was successively promoted to the rank of Colonel before eventual retirement.

James R. (Jim) Oliver, 1879–1956, son of William M. (Bill) Oliver and grandson of John and Lucretia Oliver, attended Maryville College and became a school teacher. After teaching in Cades Cove for a short while he moved to North Carolina where he taught in the Bryson City school system and also served in administrative positions for many years.

The John Anthony Family—

Some Memories

Laz Anthony, wearing the hat, clowning around with Jim and Lula Johnson. Laz, along with Witt Roberts, remodeled our home and sawed the lumber and built our new barn in 1920.

The first cleared area on the right side of the loop road, about half a mile from its beginning, was the John Anthony farm. It is identified also by a large Indian mound. Two Anthony families lived there: John T. Anthony, and his father John Anthony, Sr.

John T. Anthony's wife was Sarah LeQuire. She was a midwife. Of their

John and Elizabeth (Aunt Bett) Oliver Anthony.
Aunt Bett was the first woman I ever saw smoke!

children, I remember especially Mary, Jack, Lazarus, Laura, and Pearlle. As already noted, Lazarus (Laz) and Witt Roberts remodeled our home in the lower end of the cove and sawed the lumber and built our new barn in 1920. Mary Anthony was first married to James Everett, then to Bob Sparks, and following his death she married Uncle Preston Roberts. John Anthony, Sr. married Elizabeth Oliver, a daughter of John and Lucretia Frazier Oliver. They were known as Uncle John and Aunt Bett Anthony. He once ordered an automatic shotgun from Sears-Roebuck & Company. When it arrived in the mail, my father delivered it to Uncle John and assembled it for him. A few days later, he met my father at the mail box with the shotgun and wanted it returned to Sears-Roebuck, saying it was too complicated for him.

When my sister Lucile and I were yet small, father and mother took us

From the left are John T. and Sarah Anthony and their children Ethyl, Jack and Pearlie. The small boy is Kenneth Jones.

in the buggy one Sunday and visited the Anthonys. After lunch, we walked the short distance from the John T. Anthony home to visit with Uncle John and Aunt Bett. They had just finished their midday meal. With great interest I watched Aunt Bett take her clay pipe from the mantle, fill it with home grown tobacco which she crumbled up in the palm of her hand, and sat in her rocker for a leisurely smoke. That was the first time I ever saw a woman smoke. That afternoon, Pearlie and I explored the hills above their home. Those who have swung on a wild grape vine, grown into and securely fastened in a tree top, will always treasure the joyous experience. Of course, a vine still green must be selected, which becomes apparent when it is cut loose at the ground.

Some Who Went to War

Noah Abbott was a Civil War veteran who still lived in Cades Cove when I was small.

few Civil War veterans were still living in the cove during my adolescence.

Uncle Noah Abbott lived in the last house on the left of the loop road west of grandfather Oliver's home place.

William (Bill) Blair lived in the Spruce Flats, a community of several families located in a wide valley of rolling land about two miles east of the present picnic area in the upper end of the cove. My father's mail route extended to this outlying section.

George Washington Powell lived in the Chestnut Flats, a community of a number of families located in the southwest fringe of the cove, about four miles out the Parson Branch road from its beginning at the Taylor Whitehead place. As I remember Uncle George Powell, he was a tall, erect man with a long white beard. His feet almost touched the ground when he rode a small bay horse to Uncle Russ Burchfield's store. He had a large

George Washington Powell served in the Civil War and later had an apple orchard.

Davis Potter, who served in the Civil War, and his sister Eliza Potter Sparks.

apple orchard. Before the advent of Prohibition in 1920, he operated a legal distillery and was renowned for his apple brandy. My father's mail route also extended to that remote area. George Powell was an educated man, for his time, and once was elected as a justice of the peace (a member of the Blount County Quarterly Court) for the Sixteenth (Cades Cove) Civil District. With the passage of time and natural reforestation, no vestige remains of the Chestnut Flats community.

The George Washington (Carter) Shields home in Cades Cove is still standing. It is the next house east of grandfather Oliver's home place [Tipton Place]. Carter Shields was a son of William Henry H. and Martha Oliver Shields. She was a daughter of John and Lucretia Frazier Oliver. I do not know the origin of the name (Carter), but everyone knew him as Carter Shields. I remember him and his wife very well. My parents took Lucille and me on a Sunday visit with them. Without any disrespect, Mrs. Carter Shields was such a fierce looking woman that, as a child, I was actually afraid of her. In his book on the Cades Cove families, Dr. Randolph Shields says that Carter Shield's severe limp was the result of a wound suffered at the Battle of Shiloh. I can see him now in his rig pulled by two fine horses,

Abie Gregory and Luke Lawson.

*Mike Tipton in his
World War I uniform.*

often going at full gallop, especially when not accompanied by his wife. He was always in a hurry.

Uncle Davis Potter lived a few yards westward and diagonally across the loop road from the Oliver [Tipton] house parking lot. Reportedly, he stored his whiskey in his coffin, which he acquired and kept in his home for many years; and that he occasionally got into the coffin for a nap. But he didn't get to use his coffin for its intended purpose. I recall very distinctly one cold winter day, grandfather Oliver and I were going along Sparks Lane in his buggy. At about the creek crossing, we saw flames coming from Uncle Davis's house, which was near the intersection of the Sparks Lane and the loop road. By the time we got there the house was completely engulfed in flames. Uncle Davis Potter and his wife lost everything. He did not replace his coffin.

Cades Cove men who served in World War I were: Abie (Walter Abraham) Gregory and Alex (James Alexander) Gregory (brothers), Luke Lawson, Mike (Michael Handley) Tipton, Bob (Robert Brownlow) Wilson, Jule (Samuel Julius) Burchfield, Carl Brown and William E. Roberts. Only Luke Lawson was killed.

Ingress and Egress

Ann, Earl, and Luther Abbott taking a drive around the Cove with a friend.

There were five access roads into Cades Cove in my lifetime, all but one of which I have traveled. That exception is the Parson Branch Road, which extends from Forge Creek Road at the Taylor Whitehead place to U.S. 129 near Deals Gap, passing through the Chestnut Flats, and crossing Hannah Mountain at Sams Gap. I have been to that point twice en route to Gregory Bald via the trail that takes off there. And I have been as far as the Chestnut Flats a number of times, when substituting on the mail route one summer for my father during his vacation.

The Rabbit Creek Road connected Cades Cove and Happy Valley, leaving the Cove by crossing Mill Creek at the present Abrams Falls parking lot. When I was a small boy I went with my father on a trip to visit the families of two of his sisters—Aunt Lina (Martha Angeline) and Uncle Preston Roberts, and Aunt Mary Jane and Uncle Lee Feezell, who lived on a farm grandfather Oliver owned in the Ball Play community of Monroe

County. In the buggy, we took the Rabbit Creek Road to Happy Valley and spent the night with the Noah Tipton family. The next morning we crossed the Little Tennessee River at the Bacon Ferry and proceeded to Ball Play community. We returned home by the same route.

The Cooper Road, or Joe Road (so called because one Joe Cooper was in charge of building it) was one of the very early roads to Maryville from Cades Cove. Leaving the cove in the north side of our property, it meanders through the Chilhowee Mountains and the area where the Top of the World development is now located, and connects with the Block House Road to Maryville. The Park Service maintains this road from the cove to the park boundary as a hiking trail. I have walked from Maryville Polytechnic School (where Maryville High School is now located) to our home in Cades Cove on several occasions; then from home back to school, a weekend trip usually made in about six hours each way.

The Cades Cove Mountain–Rich Mountain Road to Townsend, used from my earliest memory until replaced by the present one, was a rather steep winding grade, beginning where the present road leaves the Cove and going through Indian Grave Gap, rejoining the present road at the Hessie's Creek headwaters ford; from there it followed the present road to the park boundary at Rich Gap and then traversed the Rich Mountain north slope, at about a ten percent grade and only one turn or switchback, to the Dry Valley community. A portion of that early road, on the Cades Cove side of the mountain, intersects the present road and is plainly visible; it was used by the Park Service as an access road to the fire tower once located on top of the mountain a short distance east of Indian Grave Gap. The present road was constructed in the early 1920s. Compared to the old road, this new one was like a King's Highway; it really made the cove accessible by motor vehicles for the first time.

The Laurel Creek Road, from the east end of Cades Cove to Townsend, went through Crib Gap and the Spruce Flats community, followed Laurel

Creek some three or four miles, and then went through the School House Gap of the Rich Mountain to Dry Valley and Tuckaleechee and Townsend. When the Civilian Conservation Corps camp was established in Spruce Flats in the early 1930s, it was necessary to practically rebuild this road from the Dunn place in Dry Valley to the CCC camp; and a road construction crew from the camp relocated the road from there to Crib Gap.

Rugged as these early roads were, they provided acceptable ingress and egress for the inhabitants of the cove, people acquainted with arduous life. Although surrounded by these great mountains, they were not, therefore, isolated or cut off from the outside world.

Arson and the
Shooting of Two Sparks Boys

J. J. Gregory playing the fiddle.
He got his son, Dana, and Wade Sparks to burn down
two barns; then he and Dana attacked and shot
Asa and Tom Sparks for injuring Earl Gregory.

In *Strangers in High Places*, Michael Frome gives a grossly inaccurate account of tragic events in Cades Cove involving Joe Gregory and some of his family, and others. I have no idea who could have given Mr. Frome such palpable misinformation. Because I lived through those times in the cove and have personal knowledge of the facts, I shall here set the record straight about those matters.

At the outset, as mentioned earlier herein, Josiah Jonathan Gregory

J. J. Gregory was angered because law enforcement had raided his moonshine business and confiscated all his moonshining equipment.

was the only son of Matilda Shields Gregory, who was the second wife of grandfather Henry Whitehead. Josiah was known as Joe, and because of his short stature he generally was referred to as Joe (Banty) Gregory. The criminal court records of Blount County show that he and two of his sons were convicted at different times for manufacturing and storing moonshine whiskey for sale. He had the reputation of making a very high grade of corn whiskey that was in great demand.

On December 8, 1921, officers from the Blount County Sheriff's office and local officers raided Joe Gregory's still, which was located near his home. In order to get the large copper pot and other confiscated paraphernalia, whiskey, etc. to Maryville, the two local officers (Deputy Sheriff John A. Myers and Constable George Brown) borrowed grandfather Oliver's team of mules and wagon to haul it to the Riverside station of the Little River Lumber Company railroad. John A. Myers was a son-in-law of grandfather Oliver and lived nearby. George Brown was working for us at the time. Of course, Joe Gregory and his family were enraged at the loss of their distilling equipment, mash and whiskey. It was known that my father

The corn crib that we managed to save still shows damage from the fire set by Dana Gregory and Wade Sparks..

was totally opposed to whiskey and had reported illicit stilling operations to the authorities in years gone by (when moonshiners' wives had requested him to do so). Joe Gregory concluded he had reported his operation to the Blount County Sheriff. Actually, Andrew K. Gregory, known as (Andy Stack) Gregory, was the man who reported Joe Gregory's still. So, believing that my father was responsible for their loss, and because grandfather Oliver had allowed use of his wagon and team, Joe and his wife decided our barn and grandfather's should be burned. She gave their son Dana and Wade Sparks $50.00 each to burn those barns. Wade Sparks, a grandson of Tom Sparks, was involved with Joe Gregory's liquor business.

On the night of December 9, 1921 there was a program at the Consolidated School. I was a participant in a debate; my father went with me. Dana Gregory and Wade Sparks followed us home. Our old barn stood about fifty yards from the road. Dana struck a match to the hay, then he and Wade walked through the fields to grandfather Oliver's barn where Dana fired the hay. We had not gone to sleep when my father heard the roar of the flames. He ran to the barn and got all the horses out except Gib, whose stable door was under the opening to the loft and where the heat

Dana Gregory, on the left, and Perry Tipton, on the right. Dana Gregory and Wade Sparks set my father's and my grandfather's barns on fire. Later Perry and Earl Gregory tried to play a trick on the Sparks.

was so intense he could not stop there. A number of cattle also perished. By carrying water from the watering trough at the branch below the house, we were able to save the crib and tool house located about thirty yards from the barn. In their excitement, one of our horses kicked me as I passed behind him with a bucket of water. We saw the flames flare up at grandfather Oliver's barn, and heard him scream. He and grandmother slept like babies and were awakened by their dog. Everything in the barn was lost, mules, wagon, farm equipment, hay, cattle. The present barn, considerably smaller than his original one, was built on the same site. My father slept in our new barn, built in 1920, for several months, fearing a return trip by the arsonists.

On Christmas Eve, December 24, 1921, Joe Gregory's son Earl and Perry Tipton went to the Dave Sparks home to visit with John and Francis (France) Sparks. Advised by Dave Sparks that those two sons were not at home but would return shortly, Earl and Perry waited. When they heard them coming, Earl and Perry decided to play a prank by pretending to arrest them—representing themselves as officers Myers and Brown. Earl Gregory and Perry Tipton were both short of stature. The Sparks boys knew that John Myers and George Brown were large men over six feet. Not being able to recognize their accosters in the darkness, John Sparks proceeded to strike Earl Gregory about the head and face several times with some object. John testified it was a flashlight. In the melee Earl and Perry identified themselves. John then took them in the house and his mother bandaged Earl's wounds and he and Perry left. Earl's condition infuriated his family; they could not let this injury remain unavenged. Christmas morning, Sunday, December 25, 1921, Joe Gregory and son Dana shod their horses, and after lunch started out to find the Sparks boys. They stopped at the home of Fonze Cable, whose wife was a daughter of Tom Sparks; they lived in the former Samuel Roberts home which was located about where the camp store is now situated in the east end of the Cove. A family Christmas celebration was in progress. Asa Sparks, son of Tom, John Sparks and other family relatives were there too.

Joe and Dana hitched up their horses, went in and joined in the festivities, entirely congenial and in apparent good humor and friendly attitude. After an hour or so, Joe remarked they should be getting home. At that, Dana picked up a wood fire poker and knocked John Sparks out of his chair and into the fireplace. Dana and Joe then pulled their revolvers and began shooting, wounding Asa and John Sparks. Calmly reloading their guns, they backed out of the house, mounted their horses and rode away and disappeared from home.

New Years morning, Sunday January 1, 1922, Tom Sparks rode up at our home and asked for my father. I told him he was at the barn. Stopping my chores at the woodpile, I followed along to see what was up. Tom asked my father to get George Brown and one of the justices of the peace and meet him at Deputy John Myers' home later that morning. When they

Sam Sparks, on the left, and John Sparks, standing, were at the home of Fonze Cable, third from the left, when they were attacked and shot by Joe and Dana Gregory.

arrived, Tom Sparks and Wade Sparks and Sam Sparks had built a fire in a small clearing near Uncle John Myers' barn. With the group assembled there, Tom Sparks told his grandson Wade to relate what he knew about the burning of the barns. Wade then detailed the facts I have stated regarding the reasons and plans for burning the barns, and how he and Dana went about the job.

About a week later, a young boy named Henry Burchfield, who lived with Uncle Ike and Aunt (Kans) Tipton, appeared at Uncle Bud (James E.) Gregory's store and bought a plug of apple chewing tobacco and a pair of cotton socks. Uncle Bud smelled a rat immediately. He knew Ike grew his own tobacco and never used any other kind, and that he wore wool socks the year around. Uncle Bud passed that information to Dave Sparks. That night officers and some of the Sparks men and a justice of the peace went to Uncle Ike's house and found Joe Gregory and Dana holed up in the attic, arrested them and took them to the Maryville jail.

Some time after Joe and Dana were arrested, and while they were at home on bond pending their preliminary hearing, it came out from their family that while they were still at large they had waylaid my father on his route with the intention of killing him when he passed by. But, as it happened, a man who they regarded as a friend was riding with my father at that point and they feared that man would be injured or killed if they began shooting at my father, and did not fire for that reason.

At the February 1922 term of the Blount County Circuit Court, the grand jury returned two separate indictments against Dana Gregory and his parents Joe and Elvira Gregory in connection with the burning of the barns on December 9, 1921. In each indictment Dana was charged with arson, and his parents were charged as accessories before the fact for inciting and counseling and hiring Dana to do the burning. On October 19, 1922 a jury convicted Dana of burning our barn, and Joe and Elvira as accessories before the fact, and sentenced each of them to imprisonment in the penitentiary for a term of 2 to 21 years. At the trial, Wade Sparks testified as a witness for the State in detail about why Joe Gregory and his family wanted the barns burned, the plan for Dana and him to do the job and the payment of $50.00 to each of them by Joe and Elvira, and how he and Dana proceeded to our barn first and then to grandfather Oliver's, and that Dana fired the hay at each place.

Dana, Joe and Elvira Gregory filed a motion for a new trial, attacking their convictions upon the ground they were based upon the uncorroborated testimony of Wade Sparks, an admitted accomplice. Judge Sam Brown sustained the motion, as I have long since learned he was bound to do, because the law is settled that a criminal conviction cannot be based solely on the uncorroborated testimony of an accomplice. We had no other evidence, and at a later term a nolle prosequi [prosecutor drops the case] was entered as to all three defendants in that case.

Both John and Asa Sparks recovered. Separate indictments were returned against Joe and Dana Gregory in the shooting cases. In John Sparks' case, the indictment charged them with felonious assault with intent to commit first degree murder by striking him with a piece of wood and shooting him. On June 24, 1922 they were convicted on that charge, and on June 30, 1922 they were sentenced to 3-20 years in the penitentiary. In Asa Sparks' case, they were indicted and convicted of felonious assault with intent to commit second degree murder, and on June 30, 1922 they were sentenced to imprisonment for 1-5 years in the penitentiary in that case. They appealed to the state supreme court in both cases, and John H. Mitchell and W. G. Wagner signed their appeal bonds as sureties. At its September term of 1923 the Tennessee Supreme Court affirmed the convictions and sentences of Joe and Dana Gregory in both cases, and directed the marshall to take them into custody and take them to the penitentiary.

Many years previously, John H. Mitchell and his father-in-law operated a drug store under the firm name of Mitchell's Drug Store in Maryville, where Byrne Drug Store is now located. As a result of a disagreement between them, John Mitchell shot and killed his father-in-law in the store. He was aquitted of that offense. Reportedly, in the intervening years John Mitchell had been one of Joe Gregory's regular customers. He was now politically active and influential. Now in trouble, Joe Gregory turned to John Mitchell, who interceded for them with Governor Austin Peay. The Governor pardoned Joe and Dana and they were back at home for Christmas 1923.

When Joe Gregory died in 1933, the family requested that my father conduct his funeral, and he did so. Ten years later Elvira Gregory, then living with one of her children in Knox County, perished when that house was destroyed by fire.

Acquisition of Property for the Park

Mama and Papa were not opposed to the idea of a national park, but they felt the amount of money offered was not a fair amount for their property.

*I*n certain quarters, my father was severely criticized, held up to public ridicule and scorn as an implacable opponent and enemy of the establishment of Great Smoky Mountains National Park. That was and is a false accusation, albeit such vilification may have resulted, in large measure, from misapprehension of the facts and issues involved. There may have been others who knowingly and deliberately undertook to heap calumny upon him and spread false propaganda simply because they could not abide any view contrary to their own. At any rate, and while there is yet time, it is important to me and the members of my family to set the record straight, out of respect for him and my mother. Needless to say, the prospect of having to leave Cades Cove, where most of their lives had been spent, where they had married, worked, raised children, buried dead, experienced joys and endured travail, was very disturbing and worried them greatly. The roots of a lifetime become deeply entwined in the heartstrings, and having them severed involuntarily causes no small measure of emotional distress. Of course, this was applicable to the other families in the Cove. Surely no reasonable person would fault any other for love of home and reluctance to surrender it.

After the Tennessee legislature enacted the statute authorizing the state to acquire land for inclusion in Great Smoky Mountains National Park, acquisition plans were set up and personnel were selected to acquire, by negotiation or condemnation, lands within a designated area. Similar plans were made and implemented in North Carolina. When land buyers for the State of Tennessee came into Cades Cove to attempt purchase of land, they represented to the people that they would be permitted to continue living on their land after the park was established. Of course, those agents of the state were wholly without any authority to commit the United States Government or the National Park Service to such an arrangement. But the people didn't know that and relied upon those promises; and a number of them sold at the price the land buyers offered. Except in those instances where the Park Service considered a home to be of historic value, most of the homes were destroyed as soon as they were vacated. Scarcely half a dozen families were permitted to remain, and as they moved away the houses were removed.

My parents were not willing to accept the amount offered by the state's agents. That was their right. When the State or an agency of government seeks to acquire private property for public use, the owner is under no obligation to accept the amount of compensation the agency seeking the property may offer. Obviously, to require acceptance of any such offer would be to allow taking private property without due process of law; landowners would have no access to the courts in such cases, and no right to or means of redress. Of course that is not the law. And just because the landowner feels that the amount offered does not represent the fair value of his land does not mean that he is adamantly opposed to the public project or use for which his property is sought. Nor should the owner be stigmatized or in any way prejudiced because he feels he cannot accept the amount offered.

When negotiations for private property reach a stalemate because the offer made is unacceptable to the landowner, the agency seeking the property files a condemnation petition in the circuit court of the County to acquire the property under its power of eminent domain. Once begun, the condemnation case takes its inexorable course to completion, in accordance with the laws and procedures applicable to such cases.

When the state filed a condemnation suit to appropriate my parents' property in Cades Cove, they asked me what attorney I would recommend. They followed my suggestion and sent me to see the late Mr. Russell R. Kramer, who was practicing law in Maryville and had represented Joe Gregory and other members of his family in the barn burning and shooting cases already referred to. Mr. Kramer accepted employment. He asked for a retainer fee of $1,000. I went home and rode a horse around the Cove to contact the people who were interested in testing their rights in court. By that time many were leaning toward the idea of accepting what the state's representatives had offered, but some made or pledged a contribution.

Mr. Kramer was of the opinion that the state could not exercise its power of eminent domain when the purpose was to turn over the land obtained to the United States, and asserted that proposition in an answer filed in the case in the circuit court. The trial judge agreed with that contention and, accordingly, dismissed the state's suit. But upon appeal the Tennessee Supreme Court rejected that insistence and reversed the trial court and sent the case back to the Blount County Circuit Court for further proceedings. The Supreme Court held that the public necessity justifying exercise of the power of eminent domain need not be exclusively the necessity of the particular sovereign seeking to condemn, and the state had the authority to condemn lands to be turned over to the government for use as a park.

State ex rel. v. Oliver, 162 Tenn. 100, 35 S. W. 2d. 396 (Feb. 7 1931).

Following that Supreme Court decision, when the case was remanded to the Blount County Circuit Court, the next step was appointment of a jury of view composed of five persons, as the law requires if requested. That was done on August 8, 1931. The duty of the jury of view is to go upon and examine the property being condemned, hear and consider any evidence offered by the condemnor and/or landowner—but no argument of counsel—set apart to the condemnor the property in question, and fix the damages occasioned to the owner by the appropriation of his property (TCA 29-16-07-29-16-113; 29-17-606-29-17-606).

On October 5, 1931, the first day of the October term, the state demanded

THE PLEADINGS.

A.

THE PETITION.

The petition is in the usual form and after showing t public purpose for which the land was to be taken a the necessity for the acquirement thereof; it was alleg as follows:

(a) The property lies within the condemnation area described in Sub. Sec. 3 of Section 20 of Chapter 54, A of 1927.

(b) It lies within the area designated for accepta by the Secretary of the Interior of the United States.

(c) The Secretary of the Interior had, by writ statement, as required by Chapter 54, Acts 1927, notif the Tennessee Park Commission that the lands descri in the petition were essential for park purposes.

(d) That all reasonable efforts to purchase from owners had been exhausted as required by said Ch ter 54.

(e) That while John W. Oliver and wife were in p session of the lands and claimed to be owners in fee, record title was such there was a possibility of outsta ing interests in others, and all such others were m parties defendant so as to quiet and perfect the title.

B.

ANSWER.

The defendants Oliver and wife defended by answer. After averring they were the sole owners of all the land and that none of the other defendants had any right or title thereto, the answer raises the following defenses:

(a) So much of Chapter 54, Acts 1927, as allows the exercise of the power of eminent domain is unconstitutional in that the State cannot exercise this sovereign right to acquire lands for the purpose of later conveying them to the United States for National Park purposes.

(b) Said Act violates Section 17 of Article I of the State Constitution in that the Act is broader than the caption and contains more than one subject.

(c) The establishment of a National Park will effectuate a change in the State line between Tennessee and North Carolina in violation of Section 31 of Article I of the State Constitution.

(d) The establishment of a National Park will reduce the area of Blount County to less than five hundred square miles in violation of Section 4 of Article X of the State Constitution.

(e) The Act is violative of Section 8 of Article XI and Section 8 of Article I in that it grants favors and benefits to certain land owners by exempting their property from condemnation, although their property lies within the park area, and is, therefore, arbitrary in its classification.

(f) The establishment of the park will except the lands conveyed to the United States from State and County taxation in violation of Section 28 and 29 of Article II of the State Constitution.

(g) Exempting the park lands from taxation will cast heavier burdens, by way of increased taxes, on lands without the park area in violation of Section 8 of Article I of the State Constitution.

The first part of the lawsuit was to determine if the state had the power under eminent domain to acquire land for federal usage. As you can see from the arguments from the plaintiffs and the answers from the court, my mother and father lost this part of the case.

a jury in the case. On October 13, 1931 the jury of view report, returned into court on August 27, 1931 was entered on the minutes it set apart to the petitioner—State of Tennessee ex rel. The Great Smoky Mountains Park Commission, all of my parents' property and fixed the value of $10,650 for the 337.5 acres. My parents, through counsel, then and there excepted to the report of the jury of view and appealed to the circuit court, both as to setting aside their property to the state and as to the amount of compensation awarded, and filed a bond for the costs. Holding that the right to condemn the property had already been adjudicated, the trial judge confirmed the Jury of View report setting the property aside to the state, and took under advisement the question of my parents' right to appeal "at this time." To this action my parents reserved exceptions and prayed an appeal to the Tennessee Supreme Court. That motion for a new trial was from the judgment of the trial court confirming the jury of view report setting the land aside to the state and vesting title thereto in the state. In that new trial motion Mr. Kramer again insisted that the state had no authority to condemn this property for the use of the United States for park purposes, and set out other grounds which in substance raised the same question. That motion being overruled, an appeal to the Tennessee Supreme Court was swayed and granted. The state excepted to the action of the court in granting that appeal, insisting that question had already been decided; and, further, moved that the case be set for trial on the question of damages since that was the only question remaining. The trial judge overruled that motion, holding that "the appeal on the amount of damages should await determination until the other branch of the case is disposed of." Upon appeal, the Tennessee Supreme Court held that questions of law decided upon appeal are settled and cannot be re-examined upon a subsequent appeal of the same case, and dismissed the appeal because it was bound by its former judgment (162 Tenn. 100) that the state had a right to take the land. Oliver v. State. 164 Tenn.-555, 51 S.W. 2d. 993 (July 5. 1932).

PROPOSITION No. 1.

The right of eminent domain is an attribute of sovereignty and is unlimited except by the rescripts of State and Federal Constitutions.

PROPOSITION No. 2

Public parks, whether acquired and maintained by the State or National Government, are for the benefit of the public, and property taken for such use falls within a proper exercise of the power of eminent domain.

PROPOSITION No. 3

As the State may, by condemnation, acquire lands for the establishment of a public park, and as the United States may acquire lands for a like purpose, there are no limitations, either in the State or the Federal Constituiton inhibiting the State from condemning land for public park purposes and conveying them to the United States to be devoted exclusively to the same public use.

CONCLUSION.

As we have seen (*Railroad* v. *Memphis, supra*) the only constitutional limitations upon the power of eminent domain are, first, that its exercise must be for a public use, and, second, that compensation must be provided for and paid to the owner, which includes due process for the ascertainment of damages to the owner.

That the act in question provides a proper procedure for the ascertainment of damages and a fund from which damages must be paid is not questioned.

That the use for which the State desires to take the land is a public one is declared in the case of *Malone* v. *Peay, supra,* and ably supported by the many other authorities hereinabove referred to.

For the reasons stated in these authorities we submit the case with the fixed belief that the lower court was in error as to the matters herein complained of and that our assignments should be sustained.

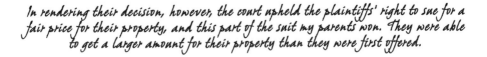

In rendering their decision, however, the court upheld the plaintiffs' right to sue for a fair price for their property, and this part of the suit my parents won. They were able to get a larger amount for their property than they were first offered.

When the case was remanded to the Blount County Circuit Court this time, counsel for the state filed a motion to confirm the Jury of View report on damages, contending that no appeal to the circuit court was granted from that report as to the amount of damages. During argument on that motion, my parents' counsel "moved the court to at this time grant them an appeal from the amount of damages as awarded by the jury of view," which motion the trial judge granted, and overruled the state's motion. The state excepted to the action of the court in granting my parents' motion and in overruling the motion of the State. The trial judge also overruled a new trial motion filed by the state and granted it an appeal to the Tennessee Supreme Court. That court affirmed the judgment of the trial court, holding that "... on this record it appears that defendants consistently demanded a trial de novo on the question of damages. Their appeal from the report of the jury of view was perfected in conformity with statutory rules of procedure" (State ex rel. v. Oliver. 167 Tenn. 154, 67 S.W. 2d. 146. Jan. 16, 1934). That court remanded the case to the Circuit Court of Blount County "for further proceedings and for final determination therein of the appeal from the report of the jury of view."

On June 18, 19, 20, 21 and 22, 1934, the case was tried before the court and a jury upon appeal from the Jury of View award of damages. The jury fixed the value of my parents' property at $17,000 and the court entered judgment for that amount. The state's motion for a new trial, and a like motion filed on behalf of my parents, were overruled, and both parties were granted an appeal to the Tennessee Court of Appeals at Knoxville on August 11, 1934.

On May 9, 1935, the Court of Appeals affirmed the judgment of the trial court, and added interest of $807.51 on the judgment, making the total judgment in the Court of Appeals of $17,807.51, and the court ordered interest on that amount until payment thereof.

In 1934 my parents purchased something over six hundred acres at

Townsend from Mr. and Mrs. Jake Farmer. Their new home was started in 1936 and they moved into it on Christmas of 1937. Their new home was well planned, modern in every respect, and they had a number of happy years there. After mother passed away, father spent some time with my sister Lucille and her husband, Charles S. Dunn, when they lived at Fort Oglethrope, Georgia while Charlie was superintendent of all military parks in the Chattanooga area. Father became ill and had surgery twice at the Campbell Clinic in Chattanooga. Lucille cared for him during his periods of convalescence. He willed her the Townsend home and some twenty acres surrounding it, and she and her family live there now (1983).

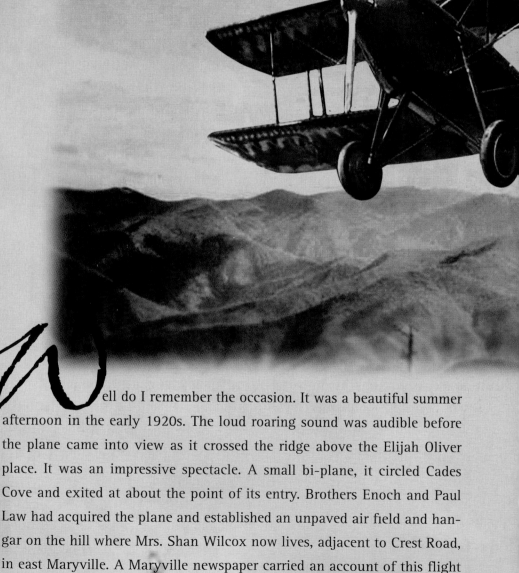

First Sight of An Airplane

ell do I remember the occasion. It was a beautiful summer afternoon in the early 1920s. The loud roaring sound was audible before the plane came into view as it crossed the ridge above the Elijah Oliver place. It was an impressive spectacle. A small bi-plane, it circled Cades Cove and exited at about the point of its entry. Brothers Enoch and Paul Law had acquired the plane and established an unpaved air field and hangar on the hill where Mrs. Shan Wilcox now lives, adjacent to Crest Road, in east Maryville. A Maryville newspaper carried an account of this flight

in the next issue. Maryville druggist John Mitchell had prevailed on the owners to fly him over Cades Cove. So intrigued was I with the plane that I made a model out of cardboard, in as complete detail as I could remember, and suspended it by a long twine string from the end of a small pole; with this arrangement I could swirl the plane in circles, and sometimes gave my cat an unappreciated ride in it. Later, while I was living with the John F. Brown family who operated a dairy, referred to herewith, when the Law Brothers' plane took off for a flight it flew directly over the Brown home.

Reverie

*O*f course it is unnecessary that today's women know how to make pickled beans, or leather britches beans, or hominy, or soap from hog grease and homemade lye (obtained by pouring water over wood ashes placed in a five foot wood ash hopper and collecting the liquid lye in a container placed under the bottom board of the tilted hopper); or how to comb and card wool and spin it into yarn and knit socks and stockings and gloves and mittens for the family; or how to weave cloth and those coverlets (bedspreads) of surpassing beauty and durability.

Nor is it necessary today that men know how to make horse shoes, or to fashion bedsteads and other furniture or to be able to make the saws and planes and lathes needed; or to build grain mills and saw mills and iron forges and smelters and fabricators, and to make their own necessary tools and implements.

But such skills and know-how, and countless others, were indispensable in the lives and times of those courageous and resourceful men and women who pushed back the frontiers seeking only opportunity—opportunity for life, liberty and the pursuit of happiness for themselves and their children and their children's children in an orderly and peaceful and productive and progressively enlightened society. In those concepts of liberty and freedom our nation was conceived and brought forth. Upon that heritage she has grown and prospered.

"The people of Cades Cove," wrote Mr. Justice William O. Douglas, "were individualistic, so much so that they kept their speech fresh and inventive.

They were dependent on their ingenuity and inventiveness to make a living out of a wilderness, to find survival for their babies, to face old age nobly. They had a faith in God that made them giants among men. The secret of America's great strength was in people like those in Cades Cove, I thought over and over again...the kindest, most thoughtful, most generous people I have known. At the same time they were the proudest and the most independent. I found in Cades Cove the warm heart and the bright conscience of America."

—*(National Geographic Magazine, July, 1962).*

"To enter here is to become one with the historic past that is our common heritage; it is to become one, likewise, with a living presence of surpassing beauty. Those whom the changing order has caused to relinquish their holdings here have given up something that is beyond price; yet their loss will be more than offset, one feels sure, if each visitor takes back to the world beyond the Cove some measure of its dignity and beauty and peace."

—(Helen & Harry James, "Cades Cove in the Smokies").

When we speak of heritage, we generally think of the culture—the precepts and customs and traditions, tenets, beliefs, mores—handed down from generation to generation as acceptable norms in human relationships essential to an orderly and peaceful society. Thus, as an example, most people understand and cherish our American heritage of liberty and freedom under law. Liberty and freedom without regard to law is license. Whether a man embraces his heritage as something worthy of emulation and perpetuation, or rejects it as imposing unacceptable restraints, it, nevertheless, in either case, has a profound effect upon him as well as upon those within his circle of influence. Much trouble and turmoil is traceable to conflicts with heritage—efforts to preserve and implement it, on the one hand, and to discard or alter or destroy it, on the other hand, depending always upon whether men believe it to be valid and reliable precepts to live by, mankind advances only to the extent that conscience becomes enlightened.

I have referred to the work at home as I grew up. My parents worked; they enjoyed work; they took deep satisfaction and joy in living by their own efforts. To them, work was not a burden or an injustice to be endured painfully and grudgingly. Instead, it was looked upon as opportunity for growth and useful and purposeful pursuit of happiness. They taught their children the dignity and essential goodness and usefulness and the imperative necessity of work, and the importance of diligent preparation. They believed in God. Their faith was firm and steadfast, and was manifested by investing their lives in trying to do good for their fellow man, and in giving their children the same vision and desire.

Those attributes of character, industry, perseverance and religious faith were not peculiar to any one family in Cades Cove. While there were a few exceptions, as there are in any community, by and large the great overwhelming majority of the people were God-fearing, law-abiding, hard-working, patriotic, energetic, intelligent, independent, deep-rooted in honor and integrity. In my time in Cades Cove there was not a divorce, and only two illegitimate children.

Epilogue

Although this history ends with my father leaving Cades Cove and the creation of the national park, his life continued at full speed. He was called to active duty in February, 1942, and served in the Judge Advocate General's Department for almost five years. During this time, he was promoted from 1st Lieutenant to Lt. Colonel and served in various capacities, most notably on the Board of Review in Washington, D.C.

After the war he returned home to practice law and served as City Attorney for Maryville from September, 1947, to February, 1949, when he was appointed circuit judge of Tennessee's Fourth Judicial Circuit. He was re-elected several times until his appointment to the newly–created Court of Criminal Appeals in 1967. In 1975 he retired to care for my mother. While on the bench he recognized the need for jurors to understand their role in trial cases. To address this need he wrote and distributed "A Manual for Jurors" at his own expense. He also began creating a manual for court clerks that Judge T. Mack Blackburn, Executive Secretary to the Supreme Court, completed in 1977. Dad took great satisfaction and was proud of his part in this project.

He was a tireless and dedicated worker. I remember his studying many evenings late at night; he was always up reading his law books when I would come in from an evening out with friends. He was also fearless in carrying out his duties as when his life was threatened in the election case in Polk County. Several times he was sent by the chief justice of the Tennessee Supreme Court to try cases where emotions were volatile.

Even with his heavy schedule, Dad had many interests. He raised chinchillas for thirteen years, grew elegant roses, and had a full acre for vegetable gardening. He was active with his church and Sunday school class and always had time for his grandchildren. He loved to take them for rides on his tractor. He also greatly enjoyed fishing on Abrams Creek and going for horseback rides in Cades Cove. His interest in education was strong; he was constantly teaching and encouraging the grandchildren. His parents

Author Judge William Wayne Oliver and his wife
Thelma Goodson Oliver.

instilled in him a love of learning as a young boy. He and my mother helped all of their brothers and sisters in their education. Some of them lived with Mother and Dad while going to college.

What was the legacy of my father? At the close of his memoirs he mentions my brothers, myself, and our children as his estate; but I feel that he leaves something greater—his humor, his integrity, his courage, his love for country, the mountains, Cades Cove and the people, and his love of us. When he met someone new, he would smile, extend his hand and say, "I'm Wayne Oliver.

Julia Oliver Webb

TENNESSEE JUDICIAL CONFERENCE

Memorial Resolution

THE HONORABLE WILLIAM WAYNE OLIVER

WHEREAS, Judge William Wayne Oliver departed this life on January 22, 1989; and

WHEREAS, he left his mark in the civic and political arena of his City, County and State; and

WHEREAS, he particularly distinguished himself as a member of the judiciary, being first appointed to the then Fourth Judicial Circuit in February, 1949 and re-elected thereafter until his appointment to the newly-created Court of Criminal Appeals in 1967, where he served with distinction until his retirement in 1975; and

WHEREAS, although he was a tireless worker, spending countless hours in disposing of his cases both at the trial and appellate levels, he nevertheless found time to author and distribute at his own expense "A Manual for Jurors," as well as a publication for court clerks, and

WHEREAS, he not only presided over highly emotional cases in his own Circuit, such as an election case in Polk County where his life was threatened, but also was sent by the Chief Justice of the Supreme Court to other circuits to try cases where feelings were equally high, and

WHEREAS, he grew from a boy reared in his beloved Cades Cove into a man of towering integrity and blazing courage, truly a giant of the judiciary;

NOW, THEREFORE, BE IT RESOLVED by the Judicial Conference of the State of Tennessee in regular meeting assembled on this 11th day of October, 1989, that we express our thanks to the Almighty for the life of Judge Oliver, and express to his family our condolence at his passing.

BE IT FURTHER RESOLVED that copies of this resolution be sent to members of his family.

Appendix
Genealogy Charts

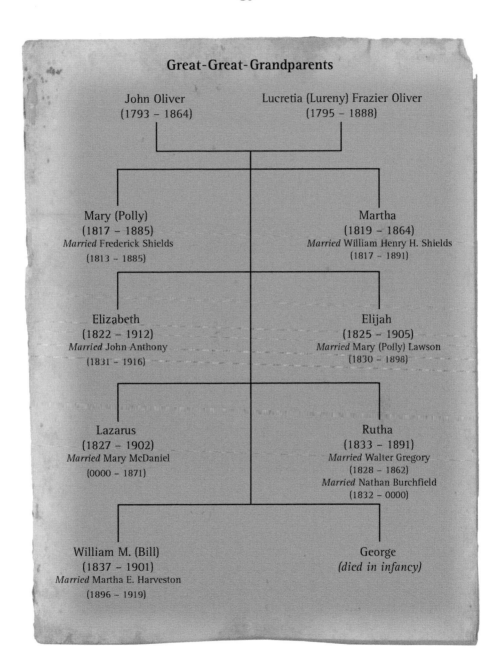

Great-Great-Grandparents

John Oliver
(1793 – 1864)

Lucretia (Lureny) Frazier Oliver
(1795 – 1888)

Mary (Polly)
(1817 – 1885)
Married Frederick Shields
(1813 – 1885)

Martha
(1819 – 1864)
Married William Henry H. Shields
(1817 – 1891)

Elizabeth
(1822 – 1912)
Married John Anthony
(1831 – 1916)

Elijah
(1825 – 1905)
Married Mary (Polly) Lawson
(1830 – 1898)

Lazarus
(1827 – 1902)
Married Mary McDaniel
(0000 – 1871)

Rutha
(1833 – 1891)
Married Walter Gregory
(1828 – 1862)
Married Nathan Burchfield
(1832 – 0000)

William M. (Bill)
(1837 – 1901)
Married Martha E. Harveston
(1896 – 1919)

George
(died in infancy)

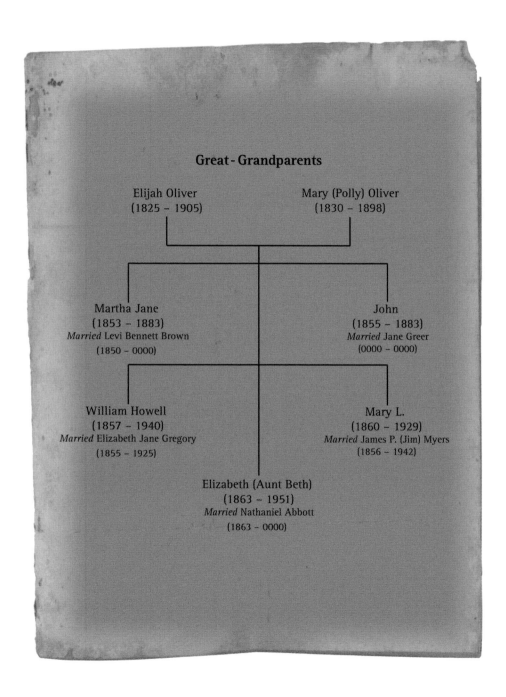

Great-Grandparents

Elijah Oliver
(1825 – 1905)

Mary (Polly) Oliver
(1830 – 1898)

Martha Jane
(1853 – 1883)
Married Levi Bennett Brown
(1850 – 0000)

John
(1855 – 1883)
Married Jane Greer
(0000 – 0000)

William Howell
(1857 – 1940)
Married Elizabeth Jane Gregory
(1855 – 1925)

Mary L.
(1860 – 1929)
Married James P. (Jim) Myers
(1856 – 1942)

Elizabeth (Aunt Beth)
(1863 – 1951)
Married Nathaniel Abbott
(1863 – 0000)

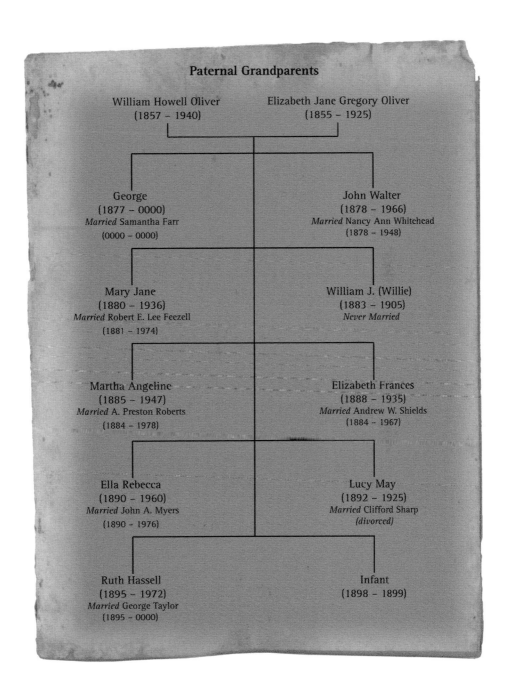

Paternal Grandparents

William Howell Oliver
(1857 – 1940)

Elizabeth Jane Gregory Oliver
(1855 – 1925)

George
(1877 – 0000)
Married Samantha Farr
(0000 – 0000)

John Walter
(1878 – 1966)
Married Nancy Ann Whitehead
(1878 – 1948)

Mary Jane
(1880 – 1936)
Married Robert E. Lee Feezell
(1881 – 1974)

William J. (Willie)
(1883 – 1905)
Never Married

Martha Angeline
(1885 – 1947)
Married A. Preston Roberts
(1884 – 1978)

Elizabeth Frances
(1888 – 1935)
Married Andrew W. Shields
(1884 – 1967)

Ella Rebecca
(1890 – 1960)
Married John A. Myers
(1890 – 1976)

Lucy May
(1892 – 1925)
Married Clifford Sharp
(divorced)

Ruth Hassell
(1895 – 1972)
Married George Taylor
(1895 – 0000)

Infant
(1898 – 1899)

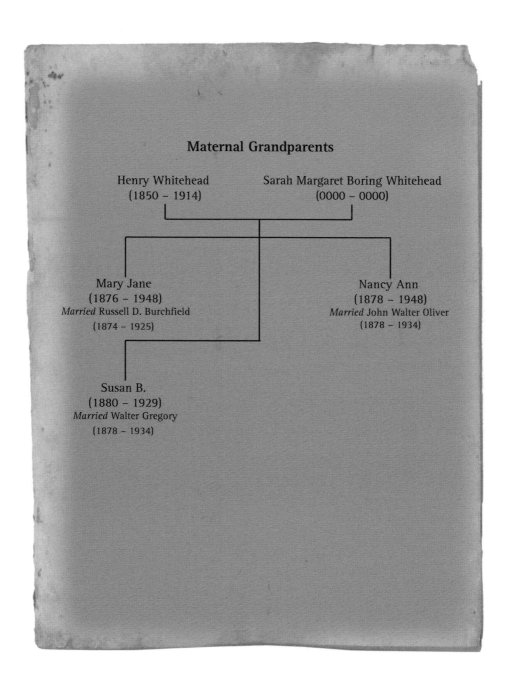

Maternal Grandparents

Henry Whitehead
(1850 – 1914)

Sarah Margaret Boring Whitehead
(0000 – 0000)

Mary Jane
(1876 – 1948)
Married Russell D. Burchfield
(1874 – 1925)

Nancy Ann
(1878 – 1948)
Married John Walter Oliver
(1878 – 1934)

Susan B.
(1880 – 1929)
Married Walter Gregory
(1878 – 1934)

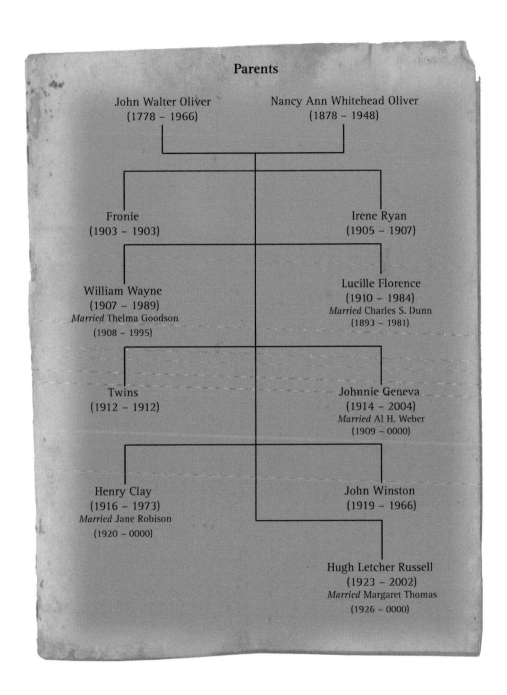

Parents

John Walter Oliver
(1778 – 1966)

Nancy Ann Whitehead Oliver
(1878 – 1948)

Fronie
(1903 – 1903)

Irene Ryan
(1905 – 1907)

William Wayne
(1907 – 1989)
Married Thelma Goodson
(1908 – 1995)

Lucille Florence
(1910 – 1984)
Married Charles S. Dunn
(1893 – 1981)

Twins
(1912 – 1912)

Johnnie Geneva
(1914 – 2004)
Married Al H. Weber
(1909 – 0000)

Henry Clay
(1916 – 1973)
Married Jane Robison
(1920 – 0000)

John Winston
(1919 – 1966)

Hugh Letcher Russell
(1923 – 2002)
Married Margaret Thomas
(1926 – 0000)